DIVERSITY

DIVERSITY

Gender, Color, and Culture

Philomena Essed

Translated by Rita Gircour

University of Massachusetts Press • *Amherst*

LC 96-279
ISBN 1-55849-025-6 (cloth); 026-4 (pbk.)
Designed by Jack Harrison
Set in Sabon with Formata display by Keystone Typesetting, Inc.
Printed and bound by Braun-Brumfield, Inc.

Library of Congress Cataloging-in-Publication Data
Essed, Philomena, 1955–
[Diversiteit. English]
Diversity : gender, color, and culture / Philomena Essed ;
translated by Rita Gircour.
     p.   cm.
Includes bibliographical references.
ISBN 1-55849-025-6 (cloth : alk. paper). —
ISBN 1-55849-026-4 (paper : alk. paper)
1. Pluralism (Social sciences) — Europe.
2. Europe — Race relations.
3. Netherlands — Race relations.   I. Title.
HM276.E7513   1996
305.8′0094 — dc20   96-279
                                     CIP

British Library Cataloguing in Publication data are available.

Contents

Preface

Diversity is about critical options and consequential choices. It is not a book with hair-splitting analyses and controversies for readers already familiar with the issues, nor is it a "how-to" book on managing diversity. I selected the format of short chapters to address women and men of all backgrounds who are generally or professionally interested in issues of diversity, but who have neither the time nor the patience to read volumes full of jargon. *Diversity* is also for students who prefer an introductory book that deals with basic notions and problems they recognize from their everyday life.

To allow the reader to understand complex theoretical considerations in an uncomplicated way, I have used many easily recognizable examples of opinions and behavior. Each chapter addresses an issue relevant to life and work in gender-conscious and ethnically diverse environments. I have been inspired by conversations with a wide group of people, including leaders and activists in various lines of work, directors and managers of schools and businesses, policymakers, program coordinators, representatives of religious groups and women's organizations, union organizers, and personnel officers. In line with the nature of diverse perspectives, I have not avoided controversial topics. The chapters, some of which are based on lectures and presentations, critically deal with racism, highlighting the problem from different angles. I also look at some of the policy interventions for addressing diversity, such as multiculturalism and positive action.

Diversity takes up issues that seldom appear together in a single monograph. I have tried to transcend the confines of specific disciplines and social and political domains.

Acknowledging diversity involves the whole person and the whole society, where we cannot separate education from identity formation; ethnic minority family life from the impact of immigration laws; the workplace from the danger of sexual harassment; racism from resistance; or policy-making from leadership. I have not tried to present a complete picture, but rather to acknowledge the scope of what it means to create space for diversity.

Diversity attempts to challenge the reader to develop alternative views on gender, color, culture, and human relations. We have a choice, and we can decide to make a society in which diversity is accepted, encouraged, and made central to human practice. Irrespective of our gender and color, we can all contribute to this ideal as responsible citizens, neighbors, parents, lawmakers, politicians, managers, journalists, personnel officers, students, or professors. Finally, it will become clear that even though the context of *Diversity* is primarily Dutch and European culture, the issues presented have wider applicability than the geographical site in which they were identified.

Acknowledgments

This book is largely a translation of *Diversiteit,* first published in Dutch (1994). Once the translation got going, I could not resist adding new chapters (1, 4, 10, 11) and revising earlier ones, in the course of which *Diversity* became a book in its own right.

I must give thanks to Ingrid Orlow-Klein for her enthusiasm at the initial stage of the project. I am also grateful to Clark Dougan for introducing me to the University of Massachusetts Press. He has been a constant source of support.

It is probably every author's dream to have a translator who is able to capture the exact meaning of her words and arguments. I knew Rita Gircour to have this ability. She had earlier translated my *Understanding Everyday Racism* (1991) from English into Dutch. I am sincerely grateful for her generosity in creating time for *Diversity.* As always: it was great working with Rita — she has a delightful sense of humor.

Last but not least, I thank managing editor Pam Wilkinson for improving the text tremendously with her scrutinizing pencil.

DIVERSITY

Introduction

Homogeneous societies are quickly becoming a relic of the past. Continuing migrations, intercultural communications, international agreements, transnational cooperations, and cross-cultural coalitions all testify to the fact that we have entered the age of diversity. Life and work in a multiethnic society comprises ambivalences, conflicts, and contradictions around the experience of national or ethnic identity. People have multiple identities and they use multiple strategies to achieve their aims. The challenge we are facing is: How can we create justice and respect between groups of people and between individuals at a time when global migrations have intensified and new community situations have emerged?

This book aims to provide basic knowledge and practical tools for understanding dynamics of gender, color, and culture in everyday life. Moreover, it examines concrete questions, choices, and dilemmas that occur in practice: How does one recognize racism? Can parents teach their children to be assertive in a racialized context? What exactly is positive action? What roles do management and leadership play in the development of a culturally diverse organization? How do women organize cross-culturally?

The first chapter introduces key notions, such as prejudice, discrimination, and the idea of "Otherness." It argues that the nature of racism has changed. A distinction is made between paternalistic and competitive racial discourses. Paternalistic racism, a remnant of colonialism, is wrapped in "good intentions" to "help" ethnic minorities. Such benevolence finds a good fit in a welfare state, such as the Netherlands, with its well-developed subsidy system. In times of economic crisis, however, benevolence gives way to hostility, rejection, and competition, and the

"Other" is perceived as a threat to the dominant norms and values. Although the focus is more on first- and second-generation ethnic minority groups than on contemporary refugees, it must be mentioned that the rejection of "Otherness" is particularly salient in the way immigration laws operate to criminalize and prevent refugees from entering the countries in the north. The increasingly rigid immigration laws, which intend to exclude people of color in particular, are in contradiction to employers' demand for the cheap labor provided by immigrants, many of whom are of Asian, Latin American, and African background. Formal policy aimed at the inclusion of ethnic minorities is, likewise, in contradiction with the reality in which exclusion continues to be a problem. During the 1980s many public institutions, including schools, universities, government agencies, and private companies, have been criticized for failing to recognize the particular cultural identities of immigrant groups. Today, the question of equal participation is on many agendas. It is seen as "politically correct" to talk about "multi-," "inter-," "trans-," or "cross-" cultural cities, policies, education, management, and other situations. Some select one of these terms to refer to specific processes of group emancipation and social transformation. Others use these terms to mean simply any exposure to difference. Perhaps the most popular reference used in this respect is multiculturalism. "Beyond Tolerance," the second chapter, exposes some of the hidden currents of multiculturalism and the norm of tolerance. It illustrates that multiculturalism operates through the explicit pursuit of cultural diversity, but without questioning the status quo of the dominant culture. The lived reality of tolerance is further addressed in "As Long as They Don't Call Me a Racist." The title of this chapter expresses the heart of the multicultural problem: management of cultural difference can become an obsession whereby individuals are more concerned with coming across as tolerant than with the quality of human relations. Practical examples of ambivalence in the face of cultural difference are taken from the daily practice of social work.

The fourth chapter also focuses on everyday interactions and deals in particular with sexual harassment. This is the only chapter with an academic orientation. It has a bit more rigor, but I tried to keep it accessible to a wide audience. The piece is relevant because it discusses a method for recognizing and analyzing sexual harassment in interracial situations. Using stories of women of color who stood up against sexual advances by white male supervisors, scenes are discussed which comprise elements of both racism and sexism. Because racism is often hidden in the routine of everyday life, dominant group members are inclined to deny the problem. The same holds true for sexual harassment, where the word of the offender is placed against that of the victim. In these situations, the definition of the "truth" depends often on whose side of the story is seen as most plausible. In order to validate accounts of experienced racism, an analytical procedure is needed to distinguish rational from irrational arguments. Accounts of (sexual) racism are not ad hoc stories but have a specific structure. Insight into the nature of the dominant culture is an important prerequisite for understanding everyday racism. This introduces questions of migration and integration into new cultural environments.

In Europe, most people of color are first-, second-, or third-generation immigrants. In the chapter on color and migration, notions of integration and identity are discussed from an experiential point of view. I reflect upon the question of what it means to leave one's country for an unknown future in another country. Moreover, when and under which conditions do immigrants develop a commitment to the new country? Questions of national attachment and detachment and of strategies for empowerment in a new home environment are considered. Arguably, some immigrants are assertive and successful in pursuing their aims, in spite of racism; others internalize inferior images of themselves. The problem of self-perception is epitomized in a discussion about the socialization of children of color. At the heart of the socialization process is the transmission of norms and values. Only a few studies have paid attention to the role of mothers (and fathers) of color in communicating norms, values, knowledge, and attitudes, which may contribute to empowering their children to face effectively the racism in society. Parents or teachers who communicate to children that the system is unfair, who give comprehensive information about racism and explain that the success of whites is partly due to racial injustice, and who also make clear that black people are opposing this kind of injustice can make a positive impact on their children. These children can be motivated to gain success for their own sake, rather than to prove that they were as good as whites, and they do not have to feel that they will forever be on the losing end. It remains a problem, however, that most schools have a predominantly white teaching staff, which deprives children of color of models to identify with in an institutional context. Matters of institutional inclusion are discussed in the chapters on "positive action" and on "diversifying," both of which address political interventions to increase the participation of ethnic minorities in the labor market and, in particular, in educational institutions.

"How Positive Is 'Positive Action' " is a critical review of the idea and practice of positive action, an intervention policy resembling affirmative action. Positive action has a number of variations but, generally speaking, it can be qualified as a recruitment strategy, whereby among two "equally competent" candidates preference is given to a woman or to a member of an ethnic minority. Obviously, it is a problem to define under which category women of color qualify and to establish whether it is even possible to perceive two candidates as being "equally competent." Moreover, a crucial difference between positive and affirmative action is that positive action is a voluntary option, at least in the Netherlands, with no sanctions or rewards attached to it. Positive action, though presented by the government as a method for facilitating acceptance of and mutual respect among workers of diverse cultural background, has a number of undesirable side effects. The idea of positive action has reinforced the tendency, among members of dominant groups, to associate the "Other" with "deviant behavior" or with "incompetence." Most important, however, positive action does not question the root culture of organizations, and thus fails to deal sufficiently with the more subtle forms of everyday racism in the workplace.

Criticizing existing intervention programs is easier than generating actual alternative strategies. It is relevant to determine which societal areas, institutions, or individuals can most easily adapt to changing demands. Specific institutions can serve as positive examples and specific individuals can serve as agents of change. The role of such agents is to analyze which aspects of the current culture hamper change, to devise methods of implementing new values, and to motivate others to facilitate change. "Encouraging Diversity in Colleges and Universities" deals with choices that go beyond targeting a number of women and ethnic minorities to be hired. Diversifying means intervening at the roots of organizations with the aim of developing a working climate free of discrimination, in which there is room for multiple contributions and talents. Opting for diversity implies creating space for questioning existing procedures, rules, forms of communication, and other things taken for granted, especially those that have contributed to making a workplace a homogeneous male culture.

The final chapters are about women of color in the Netherlands and in other parts of Europe. First, I look at pioneers — ethnic minority women in the Netherlands — who have accomplished a lot, in spite of racism. Then, I place the diaspora of women of color in the wider European context, where tendencies toward narrow nationalism compete with a desire for a transnational Europe. Europe is at an early stage with respect to developing, let alone enforcing, policies against racism. The recent war in the former Yugoslavia, the accompanying mass killings, and other violent attempts to coerce the population to concede to ethnic segregation add to the grim prospect that Europe of the twenty-first century might be controlled by nationalist, racist, and ethnicist fervor based upon racial, cultural, and religious exclusivity. The fact that women of color are located in different nation-states, at times frustrates cross-European organizing because of national variations with respect to immigration and integration policies. Yet, through media, conferences, literature, and other channels of communication, women of color recognize common experiences that transcend national borders.

"Teaching in an Age of Diversity" focuses on teaching courses on sensitive topics such as racism and investigates critical research and writings done by women on gender, race, and ethnicity. In this chapter I recall how useful critical publications from African American women have been for women of color in the Netherlands. In the early stages of (black) women's studies, there was very little research done on women of color in Europe and as a result of this lack, we learned to identify with women of color in the United States. The publications of these women challenged the sisters in Europe to think more globally and to compare local events with international situations. This experience of transnational identification has contributed to the development of subsequent cross-ethnic affiliations between women, not only with women who migrated to Europe in earlier stages, but also with newly arriving refugees, in particular those from the south. This is the subject of the concluding chapter. Referring to real-life stories by women from the Third World about the process of migration, I attempt to connect the experiences of women of color in the north to women of color in the south. To conclude, *Diversity,* with its emphasis on transnational affiliations, is a plea to transcend ethnic, regional, and national borders in our thinking and to act positively upon the challenge of gender, color, and culture in all our societies.

1
Common Sense about the "Other"
From Paternalistic to Competitive Racism

This chapter looks at what is needed for a basic understanding of what racism is about. Concepts such as prejudice and discrimination are explained, and the ways in which racism is spread through discourse and common sense are examined. Finally, an attempt is made to qualify the changing nature of racism in the period after the Second World War. Racism is a historically specific phenomenon and it manifests itself in different ways depending on the wider social structure of different societies in different periods (Hall, 1978). Moreover, different racisms are considered. The "white man's burden" idea, so typical for colonial relations, with its paternalistic, often condescending connotations, is giving way to a more competitive type of racism, in which the "Other" is constructed as a threat.

I take my examples from the Netherlands. People outside the Netherlands, in particular people on the other side of the ocean, are very often surprised to hear that almost 7 percent of the population in this small country in northwestern Europe are immigrants of color: from the former colonies in the Caribbean, from Indonesia, from (North) Africa, and increasingly from all parts of the south. Indeed, developments of decolonization, globalization, and world migration did not skip the Netherlands. Therefore, although I focus on the Netherlands, the ideas I present here have far wider applications than the Netherlands or even Europe.

The end of the Second World War marked the beginning of a period

This essay is a short, revised version of "The Dutch as an Everyday Problem," CRES Publication Series, Working Paper no 3, 2nd printing (1988).

in which ethnic groups from various backgrounds migrated to the Netherlands. The first immigrants came from the former Dutch colony of the East Indies, now Indonesia, and were referred to as Indonesians. The second group, Moluccans, are from the islands by the same name, now occupied by Indonesia. The next groups were workers and their families from Italy, Spain, Greece, Turkey, and Morocco. Finally, there are people from the former colony of Suriname and from the Dutch Antilles. The factors inducing migration were different for each of the groups and the economic and political conditions of their position in the Netherlands have changed over time. Immigrants who came during the economic crisis have been confronted with different forms of racism than those who lived in the Netherlands before the 1970s.

Ideology

Before we can discuss the changing nature of racism, we must form a clear conception of racism. Race ideology is rooted in the nineteenth-century construction of biologists and anthropologists, of different "race" categories, which were subsequently ordered as one superordinate race (Caucasian) and several subordinate ones (Mongoloids, Negroids), as the European super "race" and the stock of lesser quality, the "others." The idea of white superiority came in handy, because it justified colonialism, the slavery of Africans, and the appropriation of African, Asian, and American land and human resources by whites as the result of the inborn inequalities between the "races," which made it natural for one to rule over the others.

These simplistic ideas about humankind have changed over time. Constructions of the "Other," as well as the discourse about the "Other," have become more sophisticated. The focus on attributed biological inferiority is being replaced by a concern with culture and ethnicity. The culturalization of race is not specific to Europe or to the Netherlands. The Moynihan report (1965) in the United States is probably the best-known academic example (and ideological instigator) and represents a modernized ideology that ranks white culture above black culture, replacing biological inferiority by cultural deficiency and substituting "ethnicity" for "race." A rigid distinction, however, between the qualifications of "racial" and "ethnic" groups can be misleading. Constructions of racial (biological) categories, for instance, black, comprise ethnic subgroups as well. For instance, Afro-Surinamese,

Afro-Brazilians, and African Americans are all black, but their experiences of colonial history, language, culture, and religion make them ethnically different. This, of course, does not exclude the existence of certain cultural and religious similarities between these groups.

Today, the discourse is about "ethnicity," about "national identity," and about (post)modern cultures in conflict with "traditional" immigrant cultures. Stephen Castles (1984), who has analyzed the specific postwar conditions leading to European south–north migration, explains contemporary xenophobia and racism as strategies intricately related to the capitalist crisis. A logical consequence then would be to recognize racism in the modern context as a new phenomenon symbolized by a new name. Its new appearances did not completely replace the old forms, however, and the new discourse still bears traces of the old ideology. As yet we do not know precisely which elements of the old ideology have disappeared, how the surviving elements are represented in the new ideology, and in which constellations traditional and modern concepts of race are used as organizing principles in common-sense notions (Lawrence, 1982). Hence, the ideological changes cannot be symbolized by simply choosing a new name to replace the familiar term "racism." To give a concrete example: Dutch common-sense representations of the Surinamese vary from "racial" notions, such as "ugly, dirty, darkie" to "ethnic" notions such as "they do not speak Dutch properly" or "they live off Dutch welfare" (Essed, 1984, 1990b). Because Surinamese people have Asian, African, and other backgrounds of color, their physical characteristics, being visibly different from the "white" Dutch, remain one of the most important cognitive categories of classification. In order to acknowledge the relatedness of racial and ethnic criteria of common-sense categorization, I use the notion "racial-ethnic" in this chapter, as a theoretical classification of social groups.

The discourse about racial-ethnic groups from (former) colonies such as Suriname intricately relates to the images about groups from southern Europe and northern Africa, Turks and Moroccans in particular, that developed in the context of postwar labor migration and the economic crisis. It seemed important to develop a concept to account for the racismlike phenomena that took for their target a group of white immigrants from the south of Europe, who, because of their different ethnic background, are seen as alien and culturally backward. "Ethnicism" has been suggested as a term to describe this cultural or ethnic form of racism (Essed, 1982; Mullard, 1986). Since racial and ethnic criteria overlap, particularly with respect to the representations of other than Caucasian groups, I maintain the concept of racism as an explanatory concept of prevalent racial-ethnic structures. Yet, the term "racial-ethnic" indicates that it has become increasingly difficult to use one concept (racism) in order to account for two related phenomena: first, the ideological representations of different racial-ethnic groups that have different historical relations with the white dominant group (colonialism versus labor migration), and second, the postwar similarities in the social perceptions of different racial-ethnic groups as representing a cultural threat.

Discourse

Racism as an ideology is socially reproduced. It is communicated and transmitted through formal and informal channels. At the formal level, racism is communicated through political discourse, the media, and education (van Dijk, 1993). The informal transmission is engendered by socialization within the family, talk in the neighborhood, among friends, and in other spheres of interaction.

Some of the first Dutch studies of racial images in children's books and school textbooks came from Redmond (1980) and van den Berg and Reinsch (1983). Redmond's study analyzed one hundred children's books. Apart from a few prewar publications, her sample was taken from the period between 1945 and 1979. She found primarily "racial" representations in which African people were portrayed as "primitives climbing trees like monkeys," as "stupid," "ugly," "bestial," and so on. The more recent period covered in the study of textbooks analyzed by van den Berg and Reinsch demonstrates the ideological redefinition of racism from openly racist and racially defined forms into a more sophisticated racism that is more implicit (covert) and culturally or ethnically defined. The blatant idea of racial superiority that appears in the analysis of Redmond has been replaced by implicit notions of white cultural superiority in the material analyzed by van den Berg and Reinsch.

The reproduction of racism in ideology and social discourse has also been studied extensively by Teun van Dijk, with respect to textbooks (1987b), newspapers (1991), and ordinary conversations (1987a). The general conclusions from the studies of textbooks were that examples of blatant racism are uncommon. More subtle forms prevail, in which Third World cultures are portrayed as deviant and backward. More specifically, in his study of social science textbooks for high school students, van Dijk finds that the issue of racism in the Netherlands is almost completely ignored (van Dijk, 1987b). The images of ethnic minorities in textbooks are similar to those in the Dutch press. Minorities are predominantly presented in the context of the problems they are assumed to create for Dutch people. They are portrayed as criminals, as constant complainers, as violent, and as a nuisance for Dutch society. In addition, there is the assumption that the Dutch government pays too much attention to them (van Dijk, 1991). Moreover, their points of view on news events are considered less reliable than those of members of the white Dutch group. This is communicated in an implicit way. Their opinions are either ignored altogether or questioned, for instance, by exaggerated use of quotation marks, creating psychological distance between the perspectives of the (white) readers on the one hand, and ethnic views on the other hand. Finally, although racism is "wrong" according to norms and values, van Dijk's analysis of everyday conversations between whites illustrates how the rejection of racism coexists with ethnic prejudice. In discussions about "ethnic minorities" or "those foreigners," typical strategies such as "I'm no racist, but . . ." or "I have nothing against these people, but . . ." were used to introduce negative generalizations about ethnic groups.

To conclude, the implicit message about ethnic groups is that they *have* problems, because they are disadvantaged and that they *create* problems because they are a strain on societal resources and because their presence leads to racism. At the same time, by tolerating obviously racist political parties in parliament, the government symbolically expresses that any citizen has the "democratic" right to be racist if he or she chooses. As a consequence, the problem of racism is reduced to the level of decency and moral ethics, but racism itself is reinforced at the same time. Prohibiting a political party, even a racist one, is considered a greater violation of democracy than allowing, and therefore implicitly supporting, the diffusion of racist ideas, which, by their very nature, are undemocratic.

Prejudice and Discrimination

Racial-ethnic prejudice is an attitude, an element of common sense, based on false generalizations of negatively valued properties attributed to racial-ethnic groups other than one's own. Common sense should not be understood as a product of deliberate, systematic, and consistent thought. It is derived from and designed to cope with the routine activities of everyday life. Common-sense notions about racial-ethnic groups and related issues enable an understanding of and communication about racial-ethnic matters in the ordinary flow of daily activities. It can be argued that prejudice defined as a form of common sense does not necessarily imply an awareness of an underlying race ideology. Moreover, the dominant common sense about race and ethnicity does not explicitly adhere to a goal of confirming and perpetuating inequality, but neither does it include elaborate notions of opposition against racism.

Racism is transmitted through acts generated from a social attitude that takes the legitimacy of the racial-ethnic social order for granted. These acts, defined as *discrimination,* (re)produce the racial and ethnic inequalities of the social structure. Put another way, discrimination includes all acts, verbal, nonverbal, and paraverbal, that result in negative or unfavorable consequences for the dominated racial-ethnic groups, in particular. Thus, racial discrimination is defined in terms of acts and their *consequences* even when actors do not intend or realize, let alone pursue, the social consequences of their actions.

Indirect and Direct Discrimination

Indirect discrimination is equal treatment in equal circumstances, but under unequal social conditions. This form of discrimination usually occurs when one group, whites, are the norm group for whom institutional rules are formulated, which are then applied to everybody else, including different ethnic groups. If, for example, the company canteen fails to take into account the specific dietary needs of Muslim employees, company policy is indirectly discriminatory, as a result of that. Management may not even be aware of the consequences of the lunch facilities. They are not consciously discriminating between employees on the basis of their color, nationality, or religion. But had due efforts been made, these consequences might have been anticipated. Companies have to be aware of the specific circumstances of other ethnic groups in order to make a difference, when necessary.

Direct discrimination is unequal treatment in equal circumstances under racially unequal social conditions. It is relevant to differentiate further between explicit or overt and implicit or covert discrimination. A familiar example is "no blacks allowed in this club" versus "sorry, members only" (Essed, 1990b). Implicit discrimination deserves special attention in our discussion. Obviously, covert expressions of racism are difficult to deal with, because the underlying racism can be denied. Pettigrew (1985), discussing what he calls racial ambivalence, shows that according to his findings the denial of one's prejudice is the essence of modern racism in the United States. This conclusion may well be generalized and applied to the Dutch situation (Essed, 1990b, 1991). There are, however, ways to expose even covert manifestations of racism, examples of which are discussed in Chapter 4.

Common Sense and Denial of Racism

Let us take as a premise that people are motivated to construct positive perceptions and presentations of themselves (Goffman, 1959). In a society in which racism is morally rejected, a logical consequence of the need for a positive self image is that these self-perceptions include the belief that the self or the social group the self belongs to is not and cannot be racist. The contradiction between the normative rejection of racism and the reality in which ethnic groups, often covertly, experience racism on a day-to-day basis is solved cognitively. If racism is defined so that it excludes, and therefore denies, the covert forms of racism in particular, then society has no problem with racism. This appears to be the case. Common-sense understanding of what racism is about has little sophistication. People can explain very well that racism is "wrong," but when you ask what racism is, they will be inclined to associate racism primarily with the extremes, which are easy to pinpoint, such as the ideas of white supremacists. They are far less informed about the more complex and hidden forms of everyday exclusion. Hence, common-sense notions reject racism explicitly, while implicitly they reproduce the notions that deny, and therefore help sustain, the inequalities of the racial-ethnic structure.

The common-sense denial of racism can also be explained by the very nature of prejudice. Prejudice concerns not only false generalizations about ethnic groups, but rigid generalizations as well. This stubbornness has to do with negative perceptions of the "Other" and also with false generalizations about positive perceptions of one's own group. Allport (1958) showed that prejudiced people may have strong emotional reactions in defense of their attitudes when confronted with contradictory (positive) information about the targets of their prejudice. Apparently, information (for instance, an accusation of racism) contradicting the positive attitude about someone's own racial-ethnic group (for instance the belief "we are tolerant") produces the same effects. A few interesting illustrations are provided by reactions to my books on everyday racism in the Netherlands (Essed, 1984, 1991). White academic commentators were angered by my statement that there is racism in the Netherlands. They interpreted this evaluation of the history, ideology, and structures of power relations in Dutch society quite emotionally as an "accusation," that is, as an attack on Dutch morality. Some felt that knowledge on race and ethnic relations produced by a researcher of color was by definition "subjective," "incompetent," and even "dangerous" (Brunt, 1984, 1985). Others tried to rationalize their feelings with rhetorical, derisive, and other unacademic statements, such as: "Are we supposed to believe that if white passengers refuse to offer their seat to a black pregnant woman, or if one comments on the sturdy buttocks of a black woman, this has anything at all to do with an ideology of racism? You must be kidding!" (Bovenkerk, 1984; my translation).

A rigid common-sense belief in their tolerance makes it difficult for dominant group members to evaluate their own society with respect to the issue of racism in an unbiased way. This is consistent with social psychological intergroup theories. Pettigrew (1981) illustrated that whites tend to err in favor of their own group when explaining the behavior of black and white group members. The opposite appeared to be the case with respect to the explanation of the behavior of blacks. Because the prejudice that whites who condemn explicit racism cannot be racist actually legitimizes implicit racism in society, the *denial of racism* as a result of "positive" prejudice about the dominant group is in itself a form of racism. Below, I will discuss the structural nature of racism in more detail.

Paternalistic Racism and Competitive Racism

In the period right after the Second World War, Dutch society had to "absorb" a group of 250,000 Indonesians. The term "absorb" is used strategically here because it indicates the straightforward assimilation policies of the government. It has become traditional in the Netherlands to view the immigration of Indonesians as a "smooth intake" of a group that consisted predominantly of people of racially mixed background (Bagley, 1973; Bovenkerk, 1978). The main reason for its attributed success derives from the belief that the Indonesians never became "ethnic minorities" (Entzinger, 1984). Although I do not intend to give a complete account of the conditions under which Indonesians started to make history in the Netherlands, it is relevant to focus on an aspect that is important for the discussion of racism in the Netherlands: How were Indonesians perceived by the Dutch? This question was explored in a study by Cottaar and Willems (1984) based on the analysis of literature, newspapers, surveys, policy documents, and other historical sources. From their reconstructions it can be inferred that the "average Dutch citizen" seemed to be preoccupied with what was seen as the biological superiority of the white race. Defining the others as "unpure" (Cottaar & Willems, 100) because of their racially mixed background, citizens attributed innate characteristics to the Indonesians, such as laziness, stupidity, and vulgarity (72). Because Indonesians were primarily defined in terms of biological criteria, the idea of Indonesian culture was not an issue at that time. Their cultural identity was completely ignored by the government. Apparently it was believed that because Indonesians were already a racially mixed group, subsequent miscegenation would eventually "smooth out" the traces "of color." It seems, however, that Indonesians never really became part of the white majority. At home they treasured Indonesian family life and hid the pain caused by the abrupt severance from their beloved Indonesia. Due to a lack of studies at that time, we cannot give an account of the racism the Indonesians experienced during their arrival and afterwards. Their children have memories of rejection and verbal harassment in schools and in the neighborhoods where they grew up. When they were called "darkie" in the streets, parents told them to ignore these "stupid whites." These and other stories were seldom heard by outsiders. It was only in the 1980s that some among the younger generation openly started to reclaim their Indonesian identity (Harms & Pollman, 1982; Bloem, 1983).

The experience of Indonesians is somewhat different from present forms of racism against other racial-ethnic groups. This difference will be explained tentatively by dividing racism into two forms, which I shall call "paternalistic" and "competitive,"[1] respectively. Hypothet-

---

1. The descriptors "paternalistic" and "competitive" have been used before by van den Berghe (1967) but he used them to typify the changing nature of race relations in plantation and manufacturing economies in the United States and South America. The situation in the industrialized postwar Netherlands is completely different from those van den Berghe talked about. Therefore, I do not mean to suggest any similarities between his model and my analysis below.

ically, I propose the following components as preliminary ideas about the properties of what I call paternalistic racism:

1. Benevolent repression: racial-ethnic groups are forced to assimilate;

2. No claims for equality: unequal roles and status of dominant group are not questioned;

3. Condescending sympathy: racial-ethnic groups are pictured as childish, uncivilized, ignorant, impulsive, immature;

4. Racial-ethnic groups are perceived as *having* problems: inferiority complex, poverty, social ignorance.

The components of competitive racism may be as follows:

1. Hostile rejection: racial-ethnic groups are perceived in terms of imaginary or real competition;

2. Equality claims: roles and status of dominant group are questioned and contested by the racial-ethnic groups;

3. Antagonism or hatred: representation of racial-ethnic groups includes images such as aggressive, intrusive, insolent, oversexed, dirty, inferior, parasitic, threat to the national culture;

4. Racial-ethnic groups are perceived as *creating* problems and hence *being* a problem: they protest against inferior status, and they claim equal social access and opportunities.

The differences between paternalistic and competitive racism can be inferred, on the one hand, from the role of the dominated groups and, on the other hand, from the way they are perceived by the dominant group. In the first construction, the dominated do not challenge the racist ideology and racial inequalities, whereas in the second construction, racial-ethnic groups express reluctance to comply with an inferior status; they organize, challenge, and resist. The hypothetical concepts of paternalistic and competitive forms of racism are briefly illustrated on the basis of the experiences of four selected groups, Indonesians, Turks and Moroccans, and Surinamese. Their histories represent combinations of both types of racism.

In publications about the history of Indonesians in the Netherlands, Dutch perspectives, in which no mention is made of Dutch discrimination against the Indonesians, prevail. The idea of racism is not mentioned either (see e.g., van Amersfoort, 1974; Ellemers & Vaillant,

1985). In the few available historical documents in which Indonesians gave their own version of their experiences with Dutch people, however, we find several accounts of everyday hostility and discrimination (Cottaar & Willems, 1984). Since there was "no going back" for them, the Indonesians often outwardly displayed an attitude that seemed to accept the hierarchical and racial situation. Although we do not have any reliable information about their real beliefs and feelings, their outward compliance explains the myth of a smooth assimilation process: the Dutch did not perceive the Indonesians as a threat to their status quo (see the first two aspects of paternalistic racism). At the structural level, it seems as if the Indonesians, in accepting an inferior status, would be concentrated on the lowest social levels only. This was not exactly the case. With their predominantly clerical jobs in the colony, this group of Dutch-oriented Indonesians and their Euro-Asian descendants traditionally stood as a buffer between the native workers and the white colonizers. They came mostly from middle status positions in Indonesia. In the Netherlands, they experienced a remarkable loss of status. The Indonesians were integrated into the class system, but were concentrated in lower administrative jobs. Unemployment figures for Indonesians were as high as 60 to 70 percent in a period of economic expansion (Ellemers & Vaillant, 1985, pp. 49, 99). Probably, the Indonesians integrated into the lowest white-collar ranks at different social levels. Cottaar and Willems show that the Indonesians were characterized with such demeaning terms as "childish," "exuberant," "lazy," and so on (see the third property of paternalistic racism). Finally, the Indonesians were believed to have problems: they collectively suffered from an inferiority complex (Cottaar & Willems). Also, they had a nationality problem: they had become outcasts in the country they had left behind (see the fourth property of paternalistic racism). The Dutch paternalistically felt that they would naturally take care of this group of people who had been loyal to the colonizers and who therefore deserved sympathy (see the third property). It is safe to say that the Indonesians were probably defined and treated in terms of a paternalistic type of racism.

The predominant forms of racism are determined to some degree by the prevailing economic conditions. Initially, Turkish and Moroccan workers were recruited in a period of economic growth (the second half of the 1960s). They were welcomed as "guestworkers" under the condition that they would do semi-skilled and unskilled work. Since they were almost exclusively workers at the lowest level of society, they did not constitute a threat to the status and role of the dominant (white Dutch) group. Like the Indonesians, these workers did not (openly) demand to be treated on an equal basis. Coming from countries with extreme poverty and high levels of unemployment, they had no choice but to take a lot of exploitation, for their own survival and the survival of their families. Hence, from the point of view of the dominant group, Turkish and Moroccan workers accepted their inferior status. This suggests that in the initial period, paternalistic racism prevailed in Dutch common sense and behavior toward Turks and Moroccans. Guestworkers apparently had problems (poverty, unemployment) and the Dutch (employers) decided to "help" them. They were housed under conditions that precluded any social life, and they were treated paternalistically, being perceived as childish, ignorant, uncivilized, unintelligent, inferior, and the like (Theunis, 1979; Bel Ghazi, 1982). Guestworkers induced sympathy; the Dutch public felt sorry for them because they were doing the dirty work that Dutch workers refused to do.

The oil crisis of the early 1970s and the subsequent rise in unemployment drastically changed the economic and social climate for Turkish and Moroccan workers in the Netherlands. Also, during the same period, their families arrived. Finally, the factor of ethnicity forced itself on the perceptions of the Dutch, who beforehand tended to decontextualize migrant workers from their culture, perceptually (they were only seen as productive hands and bodies) as well as structurally (they were separated from their families and there was no institutional support for the continuation of their cultural life). From the 1970s on, Turks and Moroccans came to be perceived more and more as people who caused problems. They needed proper housing that could accommodate women and children instead of a colony of men only, which in the previous period had been sufficient. The children needed schooling, the community needed mosques, the newly arrived family members (often women) needed jobs, and so on. The Indonesians had needed the same facilities two decades earlier, but the Turkish and Moroccan workers and families (numbering about 325,000 persons) were not prepared to accept their ascribed inferior status. Therefore, they came to be perceived as a threat to the dominant role and status of the white Dutch. They organized and openly claimed equal housing, equal schooling, and equal job opportunities.

This was the situation when a large group of Surinamese migrated to the Netherlands between 1970 and 1980 (Ferrier, 1985). As Dutch passport holders — Suriname was still a Dutch colony — they could lay claim to "equal" social and economic opportunities. Earlier in this century, there had been small-scale migration from Suriname (and the Dutch Antilles): mostly middle-class families and students in search of better education. In the 1960s, small groups of Surinamese and Antillean workers were recruited for semi-skilled jobs. The planned independence of Suriname in 1975, with the subsequent introduction of Surinamese passports, made thousands of its inhabitants opt for keeping their Dutch citizenship. In the 1970s, about one-third of the population migrated to the Netherlands, most of them out of fear of political instability and to seek social and economic security. Numbering about 200,000, the Surinamese population forms the largest group of color in the Netherlands (apart from the Indonesians)!

Research findings in the 1980s show that in Dutch common-sense thinking, Turks, Moroccans, and Surinamese are increasingly perceived as becoming threatening competition. Competitive prejudice prevails. It is believed that ethnic groups get preferential treatment in housing (which they then ruin), that they live off Dutch social welfare, that they are a nuisance in the neighborhood, that they take away jobs, that they steal and use drugs, do not adapt, are socially less developed, and so on (van Dijk, 1987a; de Jongh, van der Laan, & Rath, 1984; Bovenkerk, Bruin, Brunt, & Wouters, 1985).

Turkish and Moroccan cultures are seen as particularly "backward" with respect to the role of women. It is interesting also that Turkish and Moroccan women tend to be perceived predominantly in paternalistic racial terms (sexually oppressed, passive, immature, helpless) whereas these stereotypes do not seem to be applied to Surinamese women, many of whom are descendants of African slaves (Nalbantoglu, 1981; Lenders & van de Rhoer, 1983; Essed, 1990b, 1991). These differences can probably be explained from notions of gender as a modality of racism, or, the other way round, from notions of race as a modality of sexism (see Essed, 1982; Carby, 1982; Parmar, 1982). Apart from the socially (culturally or ethnically) defined forms of racial prejudice, older, biologically related forms, such as characterizing minorities as lazy, stupid, sexually perverse (males), or sexually permissive (females), are still elements of current common-sense racism (Essed, 1991).

The above arguments support a theory of transformation of racism in the Netherlands: from biologically defined toward biologically/ethnically defined racism and from paternalistic toward paternalistic/competitive racism. The difference between paternalistic and competitive racism draws attention to the effects of racial-ethnic group endeavors toward social change. Their attitudes and actions apparently affected the reactions of the dominant group. In particular, competitive racism reveals present xenophobia and exclusion as white resistance against ethnic claims for equal economic and social opportunities. This resentment against claims for equal opportunities is a key form of modern racism as it also is in the United States (Pettigrew, 1985).

The ideological changes, from biologically defined racism toward ethnically defined competitive racism, involve a normative change. The explicit justification of the racial hierarchy in terms of sociobiological ideas has been replaced by the democratic norm of equal opportunity, even when this also causes resentment among members of the dominant group. At the structural level the social conditions changed from economic growth (and paternalistic racism) to economic decline (and competitive racism). Ethnic groups are lulled into believing that they have equal opportunities, but in the meantime racial-ethnic discrimination remains business as usual.

2
Beyond Tolerance

When you talk about discrimination in the Netherlands, people often react with surprise. Isn't Holland a shining example of tolerance? In a sense it is. Dutch society is tolerant. People enjoy a personal freedom that is virtually inconceivable in many other countries. But tolerance is not just positive; it depends on the context. One has to question to "whom," or "what," and "why" tolerance is applied. Then there is the assumption that Dutch tolerance excludes racism, which I will show to be false in this chapter. Furthermore I want to demonstrate that the ideal of tolerance is more complex than its positive image suggests. My examples come from the government policy on immigrants from the former Dutch colonies and from the Mediterranean.

Migration

Migration is a hot topic. Just open a newspaper and the headlines about refugees and asylum seekers stare you in the face. Current migrations, although they are viewed quite differently from those of five hundred years ago, are basically a modern version of an old phenomenon. Driven by hunger, persecution, poverty, the lure of enormous pieces of land, and the promise of economic growth, millions of Europeans have settled in North and South America, in Africa, in Asia, in Australia, and in Aotearoa (New Zealand) in the past. They intended to stay and took permanent European traces with them. Europe went to these places and stayed and people from these places are now in Europe. It is just as senseless to doubt the legitimacy and the rights of immigrants in Europe as to maintain that the French people in Canada should go back to France, the English, Irish, Italians, Poles, and Germans in the United

States should go back to their homelands, and the Portuguese and Spanish people in South America should give the continent back to the Indians.

The reception of immigrants in Europe has had various scenarios, according to the different policy models: assimilation, segregation, integration, and multiculturalism. These models have something in common: a certain uneasiness about cultural or ethnic difference. Cultural difference is either brushed aside (color or culture blindness in the assimilation and integration models) or greatly exaggerated (cultural determinism in the segregation and multicultural models). The models leave little room for ethnic minorities to determine the conditions under which they wish to commit themselves to the society into which they immigrated. Furthermore, the models do not, or not sufficiently, take the problem of racism into account.

Civilized Racism?

Racism in society is not the same thing as a society made up of racists, just like the "rich" countries are not entirely made up of "rich" individuals. Racism is a structural characteristic in a given society. Likewise, calling racism a daily occurrence does not mean that everyone with a "white" skin color is a racist. This assumption is not only naive, it also makes racism into a personal, perhaps even a hereditary characteristic, while racism actually is a social phenomenon.

Racism takes on several forms, depending on historical, economic, social, and political circumstances (Corbey, 1989; Goldberg, 1993). The nineteenth-century dominance of the "Caucasian race," as an idea and as a practice, always had a racial as well as a cultural component. The racial component consisted of the hierarchical differentiation of the various races, categorized according to so-called hereditary and thus unchangeable characteristics. At the same time, the idea of race was attached to a hierarchy of cultural values, celebrating European development, progress, and life style, which nurtured the cultural component of racism.

We have since learned that races do not exist and that cultures change. Still, there is the persistent idea that people of (Western) European descent are ahead of the rest of the world, and that other cultural or ethnic groups may be placed relatively high or low on the scale of human development and progress depending on their norms, values, and traditions. The cultural component of racism has now become more prominent than the racial component; sometimes it seems as though society is obsessed with real or assumed ethnic differences. People now attribute the same type of characteristics to ethnic or cultural background that they once linked to the idea of race. In common-sense thinking, ethnic groups represent another "type" of people, whose traditions are construed as an obstacle to their integration.

The "Others," people of color, have become more and more stereotyped in the dominant discourse; a threat to European culture. The creation of an enemy image, the Other, is not an unfamiliar phenomenon in European history (Hodge, Struckman, & Trost, 1975; C. Robinson, 1983; Gilman, 1985). The Other is perceived as inferior, the representative of evil against which one must defend oneself. Conversely, the superiority of the European is accepted without question. Adhering to this view implies that subsequent policies on race or ethnic relations can only mean squeezing the culturally different elements into the margins of the existing social order, or by rejecting them outright. A closer examination of the situation in the Netherlands can clarify this.

Immigration Policy

The majority of immigrants from the South who migrated to the Netherlands during the period of decolonization are Indonesians (1950–1960), Moluccans (1950–1960), Surinamese (1970–1980), and people from the Dutch Antilles/Aruba (1970–1980). A second group came to the Netherlands during the laborer migrations from the Mediterranean to northwestern Europe. They are mostly from Turkey and Morocco (1960–1970). Together all these groups make up about 7 percent of the total population, but in some large cities the percentage lies somewhere between 10 and 30 percent, with Amsterdam in the forefront with 25 to 30 percent.

The Dutch government's response to the immigration from the former colonies was quite different from their attitude toward immigrants from the Mediterranean. This has to do with changes in the economic situation in the Netherlands. Roughly speaking, there is a difference between the periods before and after 1970. Furthermore, the reasons for immigration and the positioning of the various immigrant groups in the Netherlands differ as well.

The immigrants from Indonesia were met with an assimilation policy. The assimilation model assumes that there is only room for one national culture in a society, to which immigrants will have to adapt. The policy of admission of Indonesian immigrants was decided by the immigration service, mainly on the basis of racial and cultural criteria. A division was made between those who were close to the Dutch in race and culture and those who were not. The latter were often of mixed parentage and in the racialized vocabulary of the time they were called "halfbloods." The first group (often of lighter skin color) was more welcome than the second (Schuster, 1992).

The government policy was to spread the immigrants from Indonesia all across the country, thereby actively discouraging any clinging to the sense of Indonesian identity. One can thus say that the policy of dispersion was used as an instrument of assimilation. An immigrant family surrounded by Dutch families would have a much more difficult time maintaining its identity than if it lived in a small immigrant community. It was clear to the government and to the immigrants themselves that their stay in the Netherlands would be permanent. The government wanted the Indonesian immigrants to merge socially and culturally "invisibly," as quickly as possible. There were programs to facilitate their assimilation according to Dutch gender traditions. Men could get job training, while the women were expected to take courses in Dutch housekeeping and hygienics. Nevertheless many men remained unemployed or had to accept jobs far below their qualifications. Moreover, the Indonesians were forced to put up with discrimination and keep quiet about it (Cottaar & Willems, 1984).

The Moluccan story is quite different. The government applied a policy of *segregation,* housing them in camps away from the Dutch population (Veenman & Jansma, 1981). It was assumed that their stay in the Netherlands would be temporary, because the Dutch had agreed to put pressure on the Indonesian government to give up their occupation of the Moluccan Islands (Pollmann & Seleky, 1979). However, as it turned out, Indonesia kept the islands and the Moluccans were never in a position to return to a free Moluccan state.

At first, the Turkish and Moroccan workers, who were recruited in the sixties and seventies in order to do dirty work in the Netherlands, were also segregated. Their housing conditions were inhuman, sometimes they quite literally lived in chicken coops (Bel Ghazi, 1982). The government took a passive stand: using a laissez-faire policy that allowed Dutch companies to attract cheap laborers from abroad and put them to work under appalling conditions.

In the early seventies, many Surinamese immigrated to the Netherlands. Suriname, then still a Dutch colony, was scheduled to become independent in 1975. It had gone through a long economic depression in the sixties. Almost one-third of the population opted to keep its Dutch nationality, which meant economic and social security and immigration to the Netherlands. At first, the government tried to spread the new immigrants as they had previously done with the Indonesians. But the Surinamese resisted.

With the 1980s approaching, the government launched its new integration policy (Penninx, 1979). It had become clear that a large number of the new immigrants would be settling permanently in the Netherlands. Policymakers promised "integration with retention of cultural identity." The assumption was that society could handle a certain degree of difference while maintaining its dominant culture. The integration model looked like an improvement on the cultural assimilation model. The former had meant that the immigrants had to adapt completely at the expense of their own culture. However, the question remains whether the idea of integration actually made much difference in practice. The emphasis on retaining cultural identity hid the fact that the dominant group still laid down the conditions under which society would absorb other identities. This introduced a contradiction that could not be resolved. It was hard to fulfill the promise of retaining different cultural identities on the basis of a policy that supported, stimulated, and institutionalized the norms and values of Dutch culture only. In other words, the integration policy relegated the cultural identity of the Surinamese, Turks, Moroccans, and Moluccans largely to the private sphere.

In the mid-eighties the integration discourse evolved into a multicultural discourse, wherein cultural identity became a public matter. Within a multicultural framework, cultural differences are seen as desirable and have to be institutionalized. Central to the multicultural model is the norm of tolerance of difference: mutual tolerance was to bring about harmony in society. Unfortunately the idea of tolerance does not imply mutual respect or acceptance. "Live and let live" is the motto. "Don't bother me and I won't bother you." This idea might work if it were applied to groups with equal power and equal access to the decision-making processes. It is an altogether different story in circumstances of ethnic inequality, where institutions of society are largely, if not exclusively, dominated by people of Dutch descent. As a consequence, the dominant group retains the right to set the conditions and limits of tolerance, just as in the integration model. Ethnic groups remain dependent on the consent of the dominant group in their efforts to gain their rightful place in society.

The multicultural model has also been called a hybrid model (Mullard, Nimako, & Willemsen, 1990). In a multicultural framework, the emphasis is on the acknowledgment of cultural difference, but depending on the time, place, and circumstances such recognition may be used to support assimilation, integration, segregation, or separatism. The model is therefore quite complex. And though it is a model, it is also a daily reality in which people from ethnic groups are forced into isolation (segregation) in one context, choose to align with their own group (separatism) in another context, and are pressured to completely fit in (assimilation) in yet a third context. At work the assimilation pressure is quite strong, while in education some schools offer courses on cultural difference but demand that their ethnic students adapt to the Dutch education system as a whole (integration).

All these variations of the multicultural model have one thing in common: the status quo of the dominant culture is neither questioned nor contested. The behavior of the majority is simply not a topic, and racism is not on the agenda. All these dimensions are possible in the multicultural model because what the majority says is one thing, and what the majority does, quite another. There is a discrepancy between the *discourse* about equality and difference and the *practice*, where the historical continuities of racism, neocolonialism, and Eurocentrism persist.

Cultural difference? "Fine—if we don't have to deal with it"

Acknowledgment and rejection of cultural difference can coexist. There can be an exaggerated emphasis on difference. At the same time, some do not want to be confronted with difference. These contradictions also are experienced in daily life. You have a Dutch passport, but people always want to know where you come from, why you are here, and why you are not going back. It is a Catch-22 situation. Some feel you are too westernized, others feel you have stayed too Moluccan, too Surinamese, or too Moroccan. No matter what you do, it is bound to be wrong, because what people always see in the Other is difference (whether real or imagined) and difference is primarily seen as something that falls outside the norm. I will discuss this point in the next chapter. The

"Other" can only be seen as equal when the differences are negated, but in that case the Other is no longer classified as such ("you're not really all that Surinamese to me").

The multicultural model is, above all else, a model of control. It deals with *managing* people (how do you deal with the Other) and *controlling* cultural difference (by setting limits to what is and what is not acceptable according to Dutch norms and values).

Tolerance as Repression

One premise of cultural pluralism is that the system functions most effectively and harmoniously by tolerating specific identities within a framework of mutually accepted norms, values, practices, and procedures (Brandt, 1986). Thereby, the multicultural approach tends to overemphasize the relevance of information about different cultural backgrounds as a strategy for countering prejudice. The arguments are circular and can be illustrated as follows:

1. Lack of information about the "Other" leads to prejudice;
2. Prejudice is the cause of intolerance;
3. Intolerance leads to social conflict;
4. Conflict is avoided by a mutual understanding of cultural background.

These propositions indicate that tolerance is the cement of multiculturalism. The notion of tolerance, however, is problematic. Tolerance works only under the condition that difference bears no consequences for the dominant group, whose status quo is taken for granted. Furthermore, the idea of tolerance is perceived as concerning an agreement between equal parties. The dominant group claims tolerance, which it presents as a display of goodwill. Ethnic minorities, in turn, are expected to respect the dominant group, who claims to mean well and does not want to be accused of racism. Obviously, the premise that both parties are equally tolerant and willing ignores the power differences between the dominant group and minority groups. Ultimately tolerance leads to the expectation that ethnic minorities will be tolerant of racism as well.

In relations of dominance, tolerance presupposes that one group has the power to tolerate, while others have to wait and see whether they are going to be tolerated or rejected. The ideal of tolerance, in fact a form of control, is hard to resist because the agents involved are usually convinced of their positive attitude: they honestly believe that they are doing the right thing, because they fulfill normative expectations.

In the name of tolerance, ethnic groups are objectified so that the dominant group can control the degree to which ethnic minorities can assert their own values. The language of tolerance expresses goodwill, but the practice of tolerance means that other cultures are scrutinized, categorized, labeled, and assessed by dominant norms and values: the Other must account for how they live, where they come from, why they do not eat pork, why they are wearing a veil, why this, why that. . . . Dominant constructions of cultural difference are then used to support the claim of a "threshold of tolerance" — a pseudoscientific notion meaning that a receiving country can only absorb a certain dose of "alien" culture.

The Practice of Tolerance

Because racism is often denied, the idea of tolerance has become a facade. After fifteen years of so-called ethnic minority policy, the marginalization of people of color in the Dutch job market is worse than ever, while unemployment among whites fell substantially. A sizable portion of the government's ethnic minority funds have been spent on salaries for whites. White employees can even be found in management positions in subsidized so-called ethnic organizations and on committees, councils and decision-making bodies implementing ethnic minority policy. Their demand for more information about the backgrounds of ethnic groups is growing; they hope this will help them deal more effectively with people of color.

Institutions can apply for subsidies to train Dutch employees to deal with people from different cultures. This happens primarily in the big cities. Temporary facilitators from various ethnic groups can also be recruited to help adapt services to the growing number of clients from ethnic groups. Within general institutions, ethnic niches are growing in a process I call the *ethnization* of sectors and functions in society (Essed, 1991). It is important to understand the process of ethnization to see that the principle of tolerance in fact strengthens ethnic inequality.

Ethnization involves the objectification and marginalization of specific units that are identified as "ethnic." The ethnic niches are tolerated as long as they stay marginal. So you get ethnic sports, ethnic majors for ethnic students, ethnic social services, and so forth. Ethnization feeds the tolerant self-image of the dominant group: the existence of ethnic niches is proof of its openness and flexibility. At the same time, people of color who do ethnic work in general institutions often become tokens. These institutions virtually push employees of color in the direction of ethnic work, and at the same time, that ethnic work is increasingly undervalued. When the ethnic dimension is institutionalized, white colleagues often drop all responsibility for working with ethnic groups, creating "normal" work and "ethnic" work in a context in which methods and views are developed from a white (Eurocentric) perspective. The organization itself remains exactly as it was, only it has learned to "manage" cultural difference so that clashes between the existing institutional culture and the Other can be avoided. The majority norms, without question deemed good or better, are left out of the discussion.

In this chapter, I have questioned the ideal of tolerance as applied in unequal relations. The discourse on tolerance contributes to the denial of racism and to the marginalization of ethnic groups. In practice, the multicultural model is becoming a "civilized" instrument for the maintenance of inequality. This is because:

Tolerance presupposes the power of those who tolerate.

The idea of tolerance legitimizes the construction of difference as a question of who belongs and who does not.

Tolerance does not in itself mean mutual acceptance. As a consequence the norm of tolerance becomes a facade for the marginalization of the Other.

Tolerance presupposes that the dominant norms and values are right.

The emphasis on a tolerant society hides the fact that there is structural exclusion of ethnic minority groups. This denial of racism stifles opposition and resistance.

I would like now to propose a few points that may stimulate a different direction in the way of thinking.

No Emphasis on Differences without Recognizing Similarities First

Exaggerated emphasis on differences indirectly reinforces the assumption of superiority of the dominant culture. It hardly matters whether the differences are real or perceived. Showing that dominant and ethnic minority groups also have norms, values, goals, and experiences in common may neutralize the fixation on difference. The rigid labels that cultural determinism places on groups should be relaxed. We all have more identities than just our national or ethnic ones (see Chapter 5).

Acceptance Rather Than Tolerance

It would be naive not to recognize that conflicts about norms and values can arise. This happens not only in ethnic situations, but also around gender, class, generational, and sexual issues. Tolerance of difference, however, does not necessarily lead to mutual respect. A society in which one feels valued for cultural or individual characteristics creates room for constructive criticism for all parties involved. We all have the right to desire a satisfactory existence, a right for which we are all individually and collectively responsible. Accepting this common responsibility opens up the possibility to discuss and negotiate, on equal terms, the basic premises for a more just society.

There is also a challenge for people of color to develop, spread, and stand up for their views on a just society. Is it too much to ask people of color in the Netherlands to claim just and equal rights with a bit more courage, assertiveness, and self-confidence?

No "Ethnic Minority Policy," but a "Policy of Justice"

The term "ethnic minority policy" as used in the Netherlands puts a finger exactly on the problem. It does not deal with the marginalizing aspects in society but rather with measures and strategies to control the behavior of ethnic groups. We could also speak of a policy of control. It is important to be critical of the integration and multiculturalism discourse where ethnic cultures are seen as a problem, but not the racism underlying the dominant culture. After all, it hardly makes sense to have an ethnic minority policy when there is little or no effective protection against discrimination.

3

"As long as they don't call me a racist"

Ethnization in the Social Services

Changes in a country's population structure have implications not only at the policy level but also at the level of human interaction. These forces are joined within organizations where clients come for services attuned to their specific needs. The social services are an interesting arena to observe in this regard. An increasing number of white social workers are working with clients of color (Da Lima, 1988; Deug, 1990; Brouwer, Lalmahomed, & Josias, 1992). This is a new challenge for social service institutions, which have to question whether methods that have proved effective for white clients are also good for other clients. Something that was never recognized before suddenly becomes painfully clear: the organization only has white employees. So they discuss the problem, argue about it, and finally make a decision: they will hire a new worker on a temporary contract, preferably an "ethnic" person, to analyze the "ethnic" client situation. There are subsidies for this. The project will last a couple of years, and after that, based on the findings, a decision can be made about whether ethnic coworkers need to be hired.

So the ethnic employee is hired, and she gets to work with a few white colleagues. At first everyone is full of good intentions, but it turns out that developing social services for a culturally diverse client population requires more than good intentions. Ethnic difference suddenly becomes a hot issue. The ethnic coworker notices that she cannot develop her full potential in a structure created for a white client population and a white staff. She doesn't really know how to discuss this problem without immediately getting the reputation of being a troublemaker or being called inflexible and unwilling to fit in. Conversely, many white colleagues don't seem to notice that they automatically assume that their ethnic colleague must somehow be disadvantaged and take it for granted that she cannot be competent enough to work with white clients too.

Irritations follow. More and more prejudiced remarks are heard in meetings and in the corridors. Consciously or unconsciously, the whites are closing ranks. A process of subtle exclusion begins. After her initial silence in the hope that the problems will go away, the ethnic coworker finally brings up the issue. There are bitter reproaches; emotions pour out. In short, it becomes a situation in which ethnic conflict penetrates everyday interactions and creates stress and pain. By conflict, I don't necessarily mean violence or open quarreling — although this can happen. Usually there are differences of opinion, different ways of looking at things, and conflicts of interest having to do with different positions and perceptions of reality. The white experience of having one's presence accepted without question contrasts sharply with the ethnic experience of not expecting unquestioned acceptance.

So, a management consultant is called in to give a two-day course on cultural difference. The message is clear and simple: understanding the cultural background of the Other is the key to better working relations. Later it turns out that the course hasn't helped much. The one-sided emphasis on the culture of the Other strengthens the tendency to experience ethnic groups as "quite different" and as a "problem." In the meantime, people get stuck in the pattern of thinking about other cultures as a list of stereotypes: in Moroccan households, take off your shoes; don't say "hi" to Surinamese people, but rather "how do you do, Ma'am"; with Turks, what was it again? with Dutch people, oh great! we can be our normal selves for a change. This strengthens the familiar pattern of the Dutch being normal while others are not. You always need to show understanding for those who are not normal, whereas nobody talks about the normal. It seems as though all attention is being paid to the Others and that you are always supposed to love everything about them. Having to have all this understanding can feel like pressure. Can't you sometimes be critical of the Other? But if you are critical, won't you be called a racist?

I don't call anyone a racist very easily, because that individualizes the problem. But it *is* important to recognize and take a position against practices, procedures, statements, or ideas that are hurtful, insulting, or discriminatory in an ethnic (racial) sense. That is racism, even if it comes out covertly. The less insight one has into the problem of racism, the more likely it is that only blatant and open forms of racism are recognized, which are then mistaken for excesses due to individual character defects of the offender. One gets carried away by the presumption of "once a racist, always a racist." This happens quite often, and because of it, the fear of being called a racist is real. Thus, actors become dependent on the opinion of others ("as long as they don't call me a racist"). This combination of fear and dependence fuels conflicts rather than solves them. One way to determine independently what is acceptable regarding clients or colleagues of color is to gain insight into racism. The more you know about it, the easier it becomes to talk about it without getting yourself into an emotional sphere in which one party claims to be hurt or insulted and the other is accused of being overly sensitive.

Sooner or later, social workers have to deal with discrimination: one client wants to talk about experiences of discrimination; another has no qualms about making discriminatory remarks about ethnic minorities (Cordus, 1991; Babel & Hitipeuw, 1992). Then it is important to possess relevant knowledge on the subject. Moreover, ethnic conflict in the social services is not just a matter of client relations, but also of working relations with colleagues and of power structures inside an organization or institution. Professionals can learn about everyday racism by study, by reading about the subject, or by talking with, and in particular listening to the experiences of, neighbors, colleagues, or acquaintances of color.

From Racialization to Ethnization

Ethnic conflict always has a history and so does racism. In the second half of the nineteenth century, strongly influenced by Darwin, European scientists developed a great interest in theories of human evolution. It seemed clear that having control over factors that determine progress would result in better prospects for the quality of human life. One important criterion used for evaluating progress was the degree to which a society could control nature by technology. These European scientists were not only interested in progress on a material level, but also in levels of cultural development, the so-called level of civilization. "Scientific" studies by anthropologists and biologists, supplemented by travel reports from merchants and missionaries, brought Europeans of the time to the conclusion that Europe represented the highest level of human progress (Barkan, 1992). This view was further supported by the domination of Europeans over other people, militarily and economically. Explanations were sought in the hereditary characteristics of human beings. People of European background thus promoted themselves as a "super race." Racial theories and the idea of white superiority were popular among European elites in the nineteenth and early twentieth century. Racial theory was morally discredited by the Second World War, but the industrialized world has remained in the grip of economic growth and progress. The push for progress continues, and world domination is now explained in terms of cultural difference rather than racial difference. Thereby, Western cultures and societies still count as the universal norm for progress.

The view that European progress should serve as a model for other countries is also called Eurocentrism (Amin, 1989). Eurocentrism reflects a specific kind of dualism. Although a dualistic moral order of "good" and "evil" occurs in other cultures as well, Europe adds a twist to it. Reason, high culture, and rational thought are equated with "good" while passion, emotion, and nature are equated with "evil" (Hodge, Struckman, & Trost, 1975). This dualism has often been criticized (Mangena, 1990; Schrijvers, 1990, 1993; Wekker, 1994), but it still represents the dominant framework of Western philosophy. Since the European (Dutch) norm is maintained in dualist thinking, Surinamese, Turkish, and Moroccan cultures can only be placed in the position of Other, thus representing the (undesirable) "deviation" from the norm. The way in which the principle of "good" and "evil" functions in dualistic thinking can be shown by putting together a number of values and characteristics seen as positive in Dutch (Western) culture, and then providing their opposites: For example:

Positive norm	*Deviation from the norm*
"good"	"evil"
honest	untrustworthy
intelligent	stupid
competent	underdeveloped
ambitious	unmotivated
civilized	primitive
rational	emotional
controlled	aggressive
open-minded	fundamentalist
dutiful	criminal
modest	boisterous

Prejudices about people of color in the Netherlands usually have more in common with the qualities listed under "Deviation from the norm" than under "Positive norm" (van den Berg & Reinsch, 1983; van Dijk, 1987a and b; Anne Frank Foundation & Dubbelman, 1988). Ethnic groups (and from a gender-biased point of view, women) are seen as very different. This holds even more true for groups with a Muslim background. The attributed differences pertain especially to the highly valued characteristics expected of middle-class Western European men. The word "race" no longer needs to be mentioned. The less-valued cultural characteristics are inextricably linked to color (gender) and ethnic background and are used to explain the unequal position of ethnic groups. The main problem lies in the overgeneralizations, although it is also puzzling that in this view the north as a whole is accepted as a positive norm — despite the ecological destruction resulting from unbridled profit seeking and a total disregard of nature, despite the high crime rates, the growing sense of alienation among people, and the production of warheads with which humanity can be destroyed several times over. . . .

The earlier racial hierarchy dissolves and blends with an ethnic hierarchy, while there is a shift from "race" to "ethnicity" as a central organizing principle. This change occurs not only because "race" is a scientifically outdated term, but also because Europe itself now has become a continent of migration and immigration. The existing push toward internationalization and globalization is met with nationalist sentiments and ethnization tendencies. Most Western European countries have developed from relatively monocultural European-based societies with regional or local subcultures, into relatively multiethnic societies with both European and non-European cultural variations. In their attempt to maintain the status quo, the dominant groups, that is, those who claim European authenticity, control the extent and the speed with which other cultural influences take root in Europe. The ethnization of situations and experiences is an important characteristic of the process of ethnic control or cultural dominance. With ethnization I mean that the Other is first and foremost seen as different, whereas the similarities shared are ignored. The following story shows how ethnization of experiences can happen in practice.

A nineteen-year-old from Amsterdam is angry because she has to be home earlier than most of her classmates. She complains that her parents are overprotective, and she wants to move out, but she isn't quite sure how to do this without a huge fight. She is Turkish. She thinks that her parents are strict with her because they are Turkish. This image is reinforced by stories in the paper about Muslim immigrants who are strict with their daughters and about girls who run away because they refuse to accept this any longer.

At a summer job, she works with an outgoing, slightly older Dutch girl. Imagine her surprise when this new friend vividly describes the fights she has had with her parents, their struggles, and the tricks she had to pull in order to move out. Imagine the Turkish girl's relief that overprotectiveness is not the prerogative of Turkish parents. She recognizes the experience she shares with her Dutch friend, even though she knows that there are also differences in the way they were raised.

This example also shows a second characteristic of cultural dominance: questioning the other cultures. Ethnic relations are seen as a "minority problem" rather than as the result of colonial and postwar economic and political policies of the north, or as a reflection of current north/south relations (Schrijvers, 1993). Minority policies and minority debates are designed as if by "tinkering" with minorities, they will eventually fit in. I will come back to this point later.

Gender polarization is a third element of cultural dominance. Women from all ethnic groups have to deal with unequal gender relations in their own background and in the Netherlands as a whole. Often the dominant group conveniently sidesteps the gender discrimination that women of all backgrounds experience in Dutch institutions and focuses on the problems women of color experience in their own community. Men of color, particularly those with a Muslim background, are labeled "very sexist" in the process, resulting in the depiction of ethnic women as helpless victims who must be rescued by the Dutch from the suffocating grip of ethnic (read traditional) men and their cultures. History teaches us that women — from Turkey, Morocco, Suriname, or the Dutch Antilles — formulate their own conditions of emancipation, also after emigration (von Benda-Beckmann & Leatemia-Tomatala, 1992; Makhan, Bourret, Keiserie, & Rambocus, 1990; Brouwer, Lalmahomed, & Josias, 1992; Arib & Reijmers, 1992). Still, it is often believed that Dutch institutions are more capable than Turkish, Moroccan, and Surinamese women themselves of "emancipating them" from their own groups and into Dutch society.

The fourth element of cultural dominance is paternalism, or patronizing behavior. Women's emancipation is seen as an evolutionary process, in which Dutch women have progressed further than women of color (Lutz, 1991). This view doesn't give women of color the credit they deserve; you cannot make generalizations about the development of the women's struggle from different countries and continents. It is important to take into account the influences of class, regional, and educational differences on feminist consciousness. In the last fifteen years, women's studies has become more sensitive to the differences among white women. Why not apply the same principle to the social and historical context of women's struggles from different cultures?

Everyday Ethnic Injustice

The stigmatizing of ethnic groups also affects everyday situations. But what is "everyday"? It is the things we know, that keep coming back, that go without saying in our lives. It includes most, if not all, situations in which we normally find ourselves. Commuting, tasks we always do at work, taking classes, being with the children, reading the newspaper—these are all everyday routines, as are having lunch with colleagues, making work-related decisions. Of course you can go into much more detail: a social worker's job, for example, includes a number of everyday situations, such as office meetings, consultations, visits to clients, contacts with government agencies, coffee breaks, chats with colleagues, report writing, and intake interviews. Everyday refers to routine situations, regardless of the dedication they require. It is pretty clear what is expected, although every situation has unique aspects. No intake interview or contact with a new client is exactly like any other, but the phenomenon of an intake interview is pretty standard. Most of the questions are the same and the interviewer maintains a similar position in relation to the client.

In everyday situations, we routinely make decisions and perform activities that express a preference for one option and exclude another. It is not hard to imagine how a negative, distant, distrustful, or paternalistic attitude toward people of color, or, conversely, an automatic trust in white people will influence decisions and actions in everyday life almost unnoticeably. These expressions of racism occur, without the word race ever being said.

To determine if and how prejudice is at work in the everyday interactions with clients, it may be useful for social workers to ask themselves:

Do you assume that clients of color are less able to deal with their problems and experiences? Do you expect that ethnic clients will not understand a therapist? Do you start out explaining problems by referring to cultural difference? Do you have problems recognizing similarities between clients of color and white clients? If these questions can be answered more or less affirmatively, there is probably an underestimation or lack of trust in clients of color.

Ethnic injustices occur at all levels: from shop floor to the management level, from institution to government. This is why the things that happen at the organizational level cannot be separated from government policy. Government policies toward ethnic minorities are rooted in the social construction of the white and ethnic Other as two mutually exclusive categories: those who belong and those who don't (yet). In other words, the notion of ethnic difference is crucial to ideas about culture and ethnicity in society. Ethnic difference is not a neutral concept in this. The Other is not just seen as different, but as different with connotations of being a problem, threatening, and belonging elsewhere.

Undermining Individuality and Autonomy

By the end of the 1970s, the government responded to the increasing discontent among ethnic groups with a number of what they called emancipation programs. Although the notion of emancipation sounds somewhat old fashioned, the process it stands for is still highly relevant. Emancipating groups move from a position of disempowerment into one of empowerment through a process of democratization that occurs on the basis of qualitative changes in the legal, social, economic, and political spheres.

The government claims to facilitate the process of emancipation with policies focusing on women as a group and ethnic minorities as a group. Subsidies are made available to support minority emancipation and women's emancipation, but this means that subsidies for the emancipation of women of color are distributed through ethnic organizations or (white) women's organizations. This system is not necessarily advantageous for women of color. In the mills of bureaucracy, women of color exist as an "ethnic variation" on white women or as a "female variation" on ethnic men. There is still no framework for policy-level action on the combined effects of sexism and racism.

Ethnic organizations are usually male dominated and women's organizations are usually white dominated. In the current system, women of color lose out on both fronts. First of all, it becomes difficult to get independent funding. Second, some ethnic and/or white women's organizations request money in the name of ethnic women without involving them professionally in the development and implementation situation of the intended emancipation projects.

Another problem is that employees of color are often hired on temporary contracts and among these employees, highly skilled women are frequently limited to jobs in ethnic work. This kind of work is often only marginally developed in organizations that serve the general public, and when an ethnic branch is simply added on, the organization itself does not change. These branches can be cut as soon as "ethnic" is no longer in fashion or when the money becomes tight. In such cases the women of color lose their jobs. What also happens is that women of color who were hired for general work are quietly pushed into ethnic work. Whites in the organization can then put all responsibility for ethnic work on the ethnic workers: and the end of responsibilities usually also means the end of dedication and support. So, once again, there are no qualitative changes to support the position of social workers of color. The imbalance of power remains intact. Patronizing and marginalizing the work of ethnic colleagues becomes everyday practice.

Patronizing: Subtle and Not So Subtle

A social worker of Surinamese background makes the following comment about her work in a shelter for runaway girls.

"It is a feminist organization that operates under the assumption that the only way to become independent is to break away from your parents. I have always said that this is not necessarily good for ethnic girls, because they have a different sort of relationship with their parents and families. But because I have a minority point of view, my motions are always voted down."

For children with a different cultural background, parents and family are not only the people who raised them; they are also the people who provide the necessary protection so that the children can face a racially hostile environment. Breaking with parents because of a generation conflict also means breaking with the cultural and emotional protection that the children really cannot do without. This situation, by the way, also shows that majority points of view can be repressive if the needs of the minority are not taken into account.

Patronizing is one way to "gently" force the dominant view on ethnic groups. The following example concerns a Surinamese doctor, whose story is discussed in more detail in my book *Understanding Everyday Racism* (1991). Along with her medical knowledge, she has the advantage of being able to put certain symptoms in their cultural context when treating Surinamese patients. Once she had to view a video of patients with her white colleagues. This video included scenes with a Surinamese patient. Her colleagues believed the patient was exhibiting symptoms of mentally disturbed behavior. The Surinamese doctor did not agree. The man had the "swinging" gait she had often seen in Suriname. "Typically Caribbean," she thought. "But my colleagues thought I was exaggerating." Ignoring her knowledge of this man's cultural background, a colleague was asked for his opinion. "John, what do you think of this? Haven't you been to Suriname?" Colleague John had indeed visited Suriname once. He didn't know much about all the Surinamese cultures, but like his white colleagues he felt that this man was mentally disturbed. The Surinamese doctor, by then quite angry, clearly said that it is ridiculous that these colleagues cannot see this patient in his cultural context. She was accused of being "too emotional" and of having "too much empathy" for the patient.

It is important to note that in the anthropological literature, a swinging, so-called maladjusted life-style, among certain groups of men from the Caribbean, is described as showing disdain for the straitjacket of bourgeois society (Sansone, 1992). Furthermore, critical studies show that the way society prefers to control "deviant" behavior is by criminalizing it or by labeling it a psychiatric problem (Mercer, 1986). This is completely confirmed by the behavior of the white colleagues: the swinging gait of the black man was said to be a sign of his poor mental health.

It is likely that the interaction between the Surinamese doctor and her white colleagues also contained elements of sex discrimination. Women probably recognize the "male" argument that one should not show too much empathy toward patients. The example illustrates how everyday racism works: a normal patient demonstration becomes a patient demonstration with elements of discrimination. For the Surinamese doctor, the experience changes from a work experience to an experience of sexism and racism. First, the usual paternalism toward people (women) from the former colonies plays a role: the Dutch person, in this case a man, knows best. Would the Surinamese doctor, even though she was educated and trained in the Netherlands, be thought to be more objective or competent than the white doctors if she were assessing white patients, one might ask. Second, the superficial knowledge about Suriname that the white male doctor has is seen as more relevant than the substantial knowledge of the black doctor who actually came from Suriname. Prejudice is clearly at work here: whites are objective and competent and blacks are subjective and less competent.

This example also shows that everyday events can acquire a broader meaning in the context of unequal ethnic and gender power relations. There is more to be seen than a black doctor simply saying "They didn't want to listen to me."

Marginalization

Earlier, I was talking about the misconception that European women have a head start on emancipation. In the 1980s, there was criticism of the "white" norms of the Dutch women's movement from various sides (among others, Essed, 1982; Loewenthal, 1984, 1988; Kempadoo & Loewenthal, 1986; Kutluer-Yalim, 1988). In the meantime, the idea that you cannot ignore ethnic differences in women's social work is finding more and more recognition (Da Lima, 1988; Deug, 1990; Cordus, 1991). People are now aware of ethnic differences, but the power differential between women of Dutch origin and women of color does not receive enough attention. After the previous disregard of color or cultural difference ("You're not all that Caribbean to us"), there is now an exaggerated emphasis on ethnic difference ("as Caribbean women, this is probably a totally different experience for you"). Admittedly it is not easy to find a balance between acknowledging difference — without exaggeration — and avoiding behavior that validates domination. In addition, organizations are often insufficiently equipped to deal with discrimination and prejudice in a rational manner. An (unintended) result of this is that understanding and controlling apparent or real cultural differences becomes a goal in itself, which actually leads to the repression of the emancipation strategies that women of color developed. I will give a few examples to illustrate a number of mechanisms that work hand in hand with marginalization. They come from a social worker I will call Victoria. She works in a women's organization and is the only employee of color in a team of four.

Forced to Choose between Ethnicity and Gender

National and regional organizations are advocating a progressive policy toward women from ethnic minority groups. They are given high priority among groups because of their "double" discrimination as women and as members of a minority. Due to budget cuts in the late 1980s, however, the funding for emancipation activities was substantially reduced. This led to competition between minority organizations and (white) women's organizations who hoped to attract extra funds by increasing the number of clients of color. In practice, this can result in loyalty conflicts for ethnic social workers. Victoria addresses this issue:

"A virtual war has broken out in this neighborhood, because various minority organizations are losing their subsidies because our organization has been able to attract so many more ethnic minority women. Actually, my own position is problematic. Whichever way you look at it, it is just plain a matter of money: try to attract as many ethnic clients as you can and you get a subsidy."

This blind focus on subsidies, instead of on qualitative changes that strengthen the position of women of color, keeps potential allies — women as a group and minorities as a group — divided. The emancipation worker feels responsible for women of color and tries to help them as much as she can within the confines of the organization. Victoria feels that her white colleagues abuse this situation:

"I actually work harder than my white colleagues. It is important to get women of color in here, so I go to a lot of places where they meet in order to give them information about our organization. Whenever women of color call us, with the leaflet they got from me in hand, my white colleagues place the women in their own groups — everybody always wants to get a little bit of the extra money. I don't really know how I can raise this issue with my colleagues. If I were to openly say that they are taking away my women, there will be a huge fight about it."

Ethnic Experts for Ethnic People, White Experts for Everyone

It is a positive development that there is funding to support women of color in their emancipation struggle, but there are also problems. If the funding is given through white women's organizations, women of color have insufficient say in how it will be spent — even if the money is explicitly granted for their projects. Women of color professionals in white organizations are increasingly restricted to working with ethnic clients only, which means the end of their involvement with white clients. I will come back to this in a moment.

White colleagues, however, work not only with clients from their own group, but also with clients from different ethnic backgrounds. At the end of the day, this means a double task for colleagues of Turkish, Moroccan, Antillean, or Moluccan origin, because the lack of know-how among white colleagues means that they have to work with their own clients and also have to mediate between white social workers and clients from different cultural backgrounds. This places the responsibility for clients of color not on the organization as a whole, but on the single worker of color, who is usually not rewarded for her in-house training of colleagues: "They expect a whole lot of me. They say: 'You are the expert, you know how to work with black people.' "

In a subtle way, social service work for women from ethnic minority groups is divorced from the general emancipation work. First, employees from ethnic groups are often passed over when management positions are available. Their activities are associated with ethnic and "therefore" marginal work. This situation is maintained by recognizing only the "ethnic" qualities of the social worker of color: "Because there is always so much emphasis on the fact that we are different, it begins to look as if ethnicity is the only thing we know anything about. For example, if ethnic matters are discussed during a meeting, people look at me as if to say, 'Are we saying the right thing?' On the other hand, when general items such as management issues are being discussed, nobody looks in my direction, they only look at each other, the white colleagues. So it's all very subtle."

A similar form of ethnization occurs in the communication networks between colleagues. Part of the company culture is the way relevant information or news is spread. Often, the cafeteria or a bar is the place where this kind of information is exchanged. Surinamese colleagues may not be heavy coffee drinkers; or they may consider going to a bar with their colleagues a waste of time when there is so much work to do at home; or perhaps they don't drink alcohol. Whatever the reason, it can sometimes take awhile before they discover why they are always the last to hear relevant information. It was discussed over coffee or over a glass of wine.

All these factors mean that a worker of color must be extra alert and assertive to make sure that she gets a say in decisions about general policies. If the stress of this continual extra effort becomes too much, then she will slowly slide back into the marginalized corner and she will be consulted only on ethnic matters. Colleagues often don't recognize what is going on. But they see their expectation coming true, namely that women of color are not interested in general women's matters or that they are not competent to judge them. This deprives the organization of the views and insights women of color can offer on women's emancipation. Therefore, it is important to look for a method of improving internal communication together.

Ethnic Colleagues and Ethnic Clients Lumped Together

The social worker of color is sometimes better able to assess an ethnic client's situation because the two share experiences. This does not make this colleague less professional; on the contrary, her extra knowledge adds to the quality of her work. At the same time, white social workers are sometimes inclined to identify their ethnic colleague with ethnic clients because of similarities in background. The ethnic colleague becomes, as it were, the white colleagues' standard when exploring strategies to deal with ethnic difference, but in using her in this way the white worker may forget that the ethnic worker is also a colleague who deserves professional respect: "On the one hand, my colleagues understand that they can learn something about Surinamese women from me. On the other hand, I notice that they also associate me with problems. You can see it, for example, in group discussions about Surinamese clients. They say things like 'but that's the way you people are!' or 'you people are probably used to doing these things that way.' This means they lump me together with their clients. I ask myself what they mean with that 'you people.' These are, in fact, very subtle things. I don't want to be addressed with that 'you people.' I don't equate them with their white clients either, by saying: 'Tell me how "you" whites feel about that?' "

Exaggerated Emphasis on Cultural Difference

While recognizing the contributions of coworkers of color as a positive thing, the framework within which recognition takes place makes the idea of "ethnic expert" problematic. On the one hand, it is important for everyone to be familiar with other cultures and life-styles. On the other hand, more knowledge also means the possibility of greater control. Information about ethnic backgrounds does not in itself lead to a positive opinion about the respective groups. The danger is that each expression that smells of difference will be exaggerated, stereotyped, and added to the guidelines on how to deal with, for example, Surinamese people:

"Recently we were talking, just colleagues together. I remarked that the Surinamese women I was working with enjoyed practical tasks such as cooking, or hair care. This was immediately picked up by my white colleagues and generalized: 'Oh, working on practical tasks is "the thing" for Surinamese women.' I said: 'Wait a minute. I am talking about a specific group of Surinamese women. Others may not like practical tasks at all.' The point is that my colleagues mean well. They think that if you know the other culture, you know how to deal with it, but I can't agree with that. Why do they want to codify a culture, a code of behavior for each culture, for each situation? I feel my back is against a wall. I don't understand why they want to strip us down to a few characteristics."

This quote from Victoria gets at the heart of the problem. She redefines tolerance and exposes its repressive function.

The above situations are difficult to handle because the colleagues feel that they are trying to deal positively with cultural difference. Further analysis of the problem, however, gives a different view of it. It is also possible that the colleagues are guided by a wish to fulfill the norm of tolerance to such a degree that they lose sight of the real issue: the need for both sides to adapt so that both are open to change within, and of, the institution. This process means more than adding color. It is about accepting diversity development in an organization (on this topic, see also Chapter 7 in this book). Adding color means that the organization translates cultural difference into codes of conduct that fit the traditions of the organization. This does not change its culture fundamentally, except by adding a new ethnic dimension. Encouraging diversity means changing the culture of the organization. Both ethnic and white traditions are opened up for discussion, and each comes toward each other. In this way, the nature of social work and of the institution itself both change.

Projecting a Nondiscriminatory Self-image

"As long as I don't do anything wrong!" If this is the single goal of social workers in their dealings with people of color, it may mean that they will try to do no more than objectify the other culture, dissect it, and thus control it, but will learn little from it. Cultural change in an organization, however, requires that people can accept making mistakes. If the norm of tolerance becomes an obsession, it means that intolerance or — even worse — racism is the worst "sin" one can commit. This can become a vicious circle in which people may start to act strangely and get inhibited:

"A white colleague told me that she was talking about sexuality in her client group, in which there are several Surinamese women. One Surinamese woman burst into tears. The white social worker panicked, because she didn't know 'the Surinamese way' of approaching a crying woman. Nonsense! Isn't it the most natural thing in the world to go up to a crying woman and do whatever it takes?"

The Surinamese woman naturally feels that the social worker is inhibited and will interpret this in some way. But isn't it likely that the woman would be less disturbed by a clumsy social worker than with someone who projects a feeling of "I'd rather do nothing, so no one can say I did the wrong thing."

From the above one can surmise that the participation of colleagues from ethnic groups can deteriorate into a symbolic participation. The work may be separated into normal work and core tasks (for white people) and marginal work (for people from ethnic groups). In the long run, the ethnization of work can also lead to destroying the know-how and confidence of colleagues of color in working with clients who do not belong to minority groups. Therefore, it is important that colleagues from Antillean, Indian, Surinamese, Moroccan, and Turkish backgrounds develop initiatives themselves, within the organization, to ensure that they remain part of emancipation work for white women. In addition, it can be important to form networks with colleagues of color outside the organization. This double strategy may be more demanding, but in the long run, it will bring double rewards: a powerful base of professionals of color in social work and cooperation on equal terms with white professionals.

4

Sexual Harassment in a Racial Context

Following Anita Hill's testimony before the U.S. Senate, the problem of sexual harassment in the workplace has received a lot of attention in companies and in the media. Those of us who watched the hearings on CNN were spellbound by the search for truth. It became a fascinating demonstration of rhetoric, drama, argumentation, and persuasive power.

This chapter is also concerned with testimony, but not court testimony. In the last few years, I have studied the structure and contents of accounts of everyday racism (Essed, 1988, 1991). For the purpose of this chapter, I combine sexual harassment and racism by looking at sexual harassment in a racial context. I do this by using accounts by black women of sexual harassment they have experienced from whites in leadership positions. The central question is: How do the women understand experiences of sexual harassment in a racial context and what sources of information do they use to support their assessment of the situation? To illustrate my point I use stories from women of color in the United States and in the Netherlands, collected in a research project on everyday racism (Essed, 1991).

Applying General Knowledge to Concrete Situations

It can be assumed that in order to shape a well-informed judgment about racism in everyday situations, a number of conditions are neces-

This chapter is a slightly shortened translation of my article "Ervaring, kennis en sociale werkelijkheid: Reconstructies van sexuele intimidatie in een raciale context" [Experience, knowledge and social reality: Reconstructions of sexual harassment in a racial context]. In M. van Elteren & L. Tiggelaar, eds., *Taal, Interacties en Werkelijkheid* [Language, Interaction and Reality] (Tilburg: Tilburg University Press, 1993).

sary. At the very least, one must assume a measure of general knowledge about (behavioral) rules and procedures in nonracial situations and of general knowledge of racism. In any case, racist events always imply that unacceptable practices are involved. To determine something is unacceptable one must also know what would have been acceptable, given the circumstances. In order to know whether an unacceptable event taking place in a racial context is a form of racism, it is necessary to have a certain measure of general knowledge about racism. I cannot here explore how one acquires knowledge about racism, but I will discuss the use of that knowledge in the interpretation of everyday experiences (Essed, 1991). By way of examples, I will reconstruct two accounts of a similar event. In both cases, the accounts are those of an African American student dealing with a white male professor who cannot keep his hands to himself.

The first story concerns a woman I will call Denise. She is twenty-one years old and tells of an event that happened a few years ago. During the interview, she says that she has never had any real involvement with racism. She has, she says, only recently "discovered" that she is black and does not really know what the culture and experience of black people are. She grew up in a strongly religious environment as a child in the only African American family in the neighborhood. She learned from her mother that "there's no such thing as color in the eyes of God" and that everyone is equal. She has recently discovered that in reality this is not the case. This first example will show the problems that occur when relevant general knowledge is absent.

I will call the second woman Angela. She is in her late twenties. She also talks about an event that took place a few years ago. She has been more deeply involved with the problem of racism and tells her story using knowledge she has acquired about racism.

Shortened and edited, their stories are as follows: Denise tells of a professor who was about fifty years old. She was having trouble with her mathematics exams. He says "it is fine" for her to come to "his office" and that he "will help her." Once she is in his office, he starts making remarks like "You're attractive" and "I would like to see you." Denise doesn't respond. She continues to come because she really needs the extra help. One day "he was trying to kiss me." When she resists, he reproaches her "Well I know you like this. Don't pretend you don't" and "You know you started the whole thing." Shocked, she asks herself what she has done to give this man the impression that she wants to be sexual with him. She decides not to go to his office anymore and fails the next exams. Then she quits school. She registers at another "junior college" and is asked to see the "EOP adviser" (Equal Opportunity Program) — a black man. During that conversation, everything that happened at the other school comes out. The officer tells her that she shouldn't blame herself because there are a lot of white men who feel that black women are there to be used sexually, and that they can get away with it. This information is news to her, but it certainly did "sort of click," says Denise.

A detailed analysis of this account can be found in Essed (1991). What is important here is that Denise, who did not define herself as a black woman, was hardly aware of sexual stereotyping of black women in the United States, had little knowledge of patterns of racial discrimination, and did not see the situation in that context. The story Denise told includes no general knowledge of either sexual intimidation (or sexism in general), or racism. She did interpret the professor's behavior as unacceptable, but without a larger explanatory framework she had no recourse but to seek an explanation in her own behavior. The EOP officer explained the story as an abuse of functional power (dependent student, teacher with power) in a manner that actualizes both the gender and the racial context (white men who think that black women exist for their sexual needs). From this account we can infer that he also employed abstract knowledge of racism in his interpretation, specifically insight into stereotypes of black women as sexually available.

Angela had more or less the same experience. However, she strongly emphasizes the racist implications of a situation in which she was harassed by a white professor. She also activates abstract notions of racism in the interpretation process. Her story is about a professor in environmental science. A group of students had a project discussion over dinner at his home. Afterward, she was the last one remaining to finish up a few things. While they were talking and clearing the table, he "suddenly began to kiss" her. He remarked that they "could spend a nice evening together." Angela suspected that he thought "this sort of thing isn't anything new" for her, and that he believed that because she "was black she was easy to get, like a whore." Angry that he abused the situation, is "older," and "not at all attractive," she pushed him away with a decisive "NO." She immediately started to leave. He got into a "rage" going on about "how dare she reject him."

Is this just sexism or is it also racism? Some elements of these stories shed light on the significance we can give to the events. In my opinion, the gender context in these encounters cannot be separated from the racial context, because images of women's sexuality are racially/ethnically structured. One cannot perceive of "women" as a category without noting class, age, ethnicity, and racial backgrounds. The student is a woman and black. Thus her experience must be seen in light of the historical sexual abuse and contemporary representations of black women's sexuality. The professor is not just a man, but also white. Regardless of his interpretation of the situation, his behavior cannot be taken out of the wider (historically developed) context in which men in the dominant group appropriate control over the sexuality of women in the dominated group. The professor can confirm or reject the wider context with his behavior. His actual behavior sustains it more than rejects it. Angela's interpretation agrees with that of the EOP officer in Denise's case. In referring to the "black woman who is seen as a whore" and to the "white man who sexually abuses black women," both refer to a certain set of racist ideas that are specific to the (history of) racial discrimination in the United States. As researchers, we can use documentation to delineate a larger framework of relevant general knowledge of the sociopolitical context of both situations.

The Historical and Social Context

Increasingly, critical studies agree that race/ethnic, gender, and class systems are linked and determine the nature of black women's experience (Collins, 1990; hooks, 1989). Therefore a general knowledge of sexism is necessary, but it is not in itself sufficient to understand sexual harassment of black women by white men. In the history of European dominance, black women have been the object of economic and sexual exploitation. Black women in the United States, the Caribbean, and the African colonies have found many ways to resist the degradation of slavery (Hine & Wittenstein, 1985). They had little protection against slaveholders who sexually molested them as has been documented in various studies (Davis, 1981; Fox-Genovese, 1988; Gutman, 1976; Jones, 1985), in slave narratives (for instance Brent, 1973) and in novels (Carby, 1987). The sexual abuse of black women was ideologically legitimated by depicting them as animals, close to nature, and promiscuous. This was true not only in the United States, but also under the Dutch system of slavery (Oomens, 1986). One important difference between the European continent and the United States is that sexual abuse of black women is not rooted in social relations on the continent itself, but in the overseas colonies. Stereotypes about the sexuality of black people have remained part of European and North American consciousness (Hoch, 1979; Gilman, 1985; Stember, 1976). Sexual violence against black women has also remained an essential part of the system of racism (Lerner, 1973; White, 1985; Rollins, 1985; Carby, 1987). The sexual objectification of women served to perpetuate a double standard in which women were either madonna or whore. Both of these images were in fact racialized, where the madonna-type came to be associated exclusively with white women. The whore-type, however, was associated with a specific category of white women (the "fallen women") and further, with *all* black women. Black women in the United States are usually aware of the existing stereotypes and how they came to be. For these reasons, among others, they are often reluctant to respond to advances by white men (Staples, 1976).

The situation in the Netherlands is more complex. As is true in the United States, Dutch stereotypical notions of the sexuality of African women goes back a few centuries (Paasman, 1987; Nederveen-Pieterse, 1990), although the integration of such images into current social relations in the Netherlands is much more recent, probably dating from the postwar years, when people from the colonies came to the Netherlands. I intentionally speak about the colonies in general, rather than specifically about people of African origin. Little is known about the constructions of the sexuality of women of African origin, but these constructions probably cannot be perceived without viewing them against colonial images of the sexuality of other women in the (then-) Dutch overseas territories in Indonesia and the Caribbean. These connotations were, and still are, also related to notions of "exotic" sexuality. Furthermore, due to the frequent communication of images in the United States media, it is not unlikely that dominant United States stereotypes about black women also play a role in the Netherlands.

The Structure of Accounts of Racism

Accounts of racism construct events that evoke indignation or rejection and are seen as unacceptable. By definition, these reconstructions include descriptive information (who—what—when), but they may also include explanatory (why) or persuasive elements to support interpretations.

My method of analyzing accounts of racism is more broadly discussed and applied elsewhere (Essed, 1988; Louw-Potgieter, 1989), which I will only summarize here. It is of crucial importance to mention that the accounts always contain information about practices that are not acceptable in a given situation. The evaluation that it is an instance of racism occurs by *inference* (from general knowledge of racism, expectations, opinions, and so on), whether or not they are supported by further argumentation, using information on the basis of *comparison* (with other situations, experiences of other blacks, etc.). The categories I give here can hypothetically be seen as elements of accounts of experiences of racism:

1. *Context:* When, where, who was involved?
2. *Complication:* What went wrong?
3. *Evaluation:* Was it racism?
4. *Argumentation:* Why do you think it was racism?
5. *Decision:* How did you react, or how did you want to react to the situation?

The Context, Complication, and Decision are *constant* elements in the structure of accounts. They are the facts of the situation, as experienced, and form the core of the account. By this I do not mean to suggest that the speaker can always remember all the relevant information at any time. Furthermore, the speaker can decide whether to provide certain information. The Evaluation and Argumentation contain *variable* information. After all, interpretations and points of view can change. In earlier publications I discuss the structure of accounts of racism schematically and explain the connection between the different categories. Here I will illustrate the categories indicated above with a concrete example. The order of presentation of the categories is pragmatic and does not necessarily run parallel to the account. My example is taken from an interview with Marisca, a Dutch student of Surinamese background. Her family migrated to the Netherlands when she was four years old. Marisca witnessed sexual harassment against another colleague of Surinamese origin. We will call her Sita.

1. *The Context:* This category contains information about the time, place, people, and social circumstances of the event: Marisca was working as a temporary employee at the central telephone reception office of a bank. One day, Sita came into the building with her boss walking right behind her. Both were coming back from lunch.

2. *The Complication:* This category includes an unexpected occurrence that breaks the expected routine. More precisely, it is a nonacceptable intervention in the situation. Being able to identify irregular behavior — in our case sexual harassment — means that the speaker is informed about the "normal" course of things and thus has relevant knowledge of rules and procedures in the dominant culture. "Normal" is in quotation marks because the definition of procedures, rules, and behavioral codes in a (sub)culture can differ depending upon the situation. It is even more complex because more or less subtle forms of sexual harassment can belong to an informal company culture as if "normal," though such practices are formally rejected. The Complication in Marisca's account is an illustration of sexual harassment against Sita. While Sita and her boss walk into the building, "he 'just' grabs her breast," Marisca reports.

3. *The Evaluation:* The Evaluation includes an opinion about what happened. In accounts of racism the only further thing of interest is whether, in the opinion of the speaker, it is an instance of racism. Marisca, in her version of what occurred, did not go into Sita's evaluation of the event. Marisca herself offered this account as one clear example in a series, brought up to illustrate the following statement: "I have only experienced one clear form of discrimination. The rest was more subtle."

4. *The Argumentation (1):* This category is actually an extension of the Evaluation. It serves to support it. In order to understand Marisca's interpretation of the situation, I will go to the last category first: reaction to the event.

5. *The Decision:* This category indicates a reaction to the Complication. It can be an action or a lack of action. It can also be a feeling or a point of view (for instance: "I got really angry"). Here, two reactions are relevant: Sita's and Marisca's. Sita reacts, new Complications appear, and she again reacts. This is the sequence: Decision — Sita "steps back and pops him one." Then the second Complication occurs. The boss orders her into his office and "teaches her a lesson." The Decision of this event is that Sita goes to the branch manager with a complaint. The manager "makes a big deal of it" because it "really went too far." Here is another Complication. Her boss, who stands under the manager in the branch hierarchy, lays the blame on Sita herself, saying she

had "provoked it" because "the darker girls are always so frivolous, wiggling their ass a little and dressing nicely and 'hahaha and spontaneous' and one isn't insensitive to that sort of thing." Sita finds the accusation "ridiculous." Obviously, the branch manager agrees. One part of the story ends in a Decision. The boss gets a reprimand. But the atmosphere is spoiled to such a degree that Sita leaves soon after. There is another Decision in the account. Marisca too reacts to the situation. One of her responses is emotional: she is "furious." Other reactions influence actions toward the boss and toward the temporary agency. She "does not talk to him anymore" and lodges a complaint at the temporary agency. They can't do anything for Sita, because she isn't a temporary worker. Marisca asks that in the future "no black temporary help" be sent to the bank "because that man may become a problem again." The temporary agency reassures her. They promise to "intervene" if necessary.

4. *Argumentation (2):* Let us now return to the Argumentation category. The function of this category is to support the Evaluation that there was sexual harassment containing racial/ethnic factors. The Argumentation category is based on two methods of interpretation: first, inference—from opinions, expectations, and knowledge about racial issues and racism, and second, comparison—for (in)consistency and consensus. The following questions can serve as guidelines for inference and comparison:

1. Has the boss done something similar before with black employees? Compare similar experiences of other black women, or similar situations with the same person (consistency).

2. Was it the first time the boss molested Sita? Compare other experiences with the same person (consistency).

3. Has Marisca (or another black woman) also experienced something similar? Compare experiences with other white men (or black women), in similar or different situations (consistency).

4. Did the boss admit that he did what he did (among other reasons) because of Sita's racial/ethnic heritage? Confirm (or extract a confession) with or from the person himself (consensus).

5. Has Sita (or Marisca) spoken to others about this and what was their opinion? Gain affirmation from others about the event/about the person (consensus).

6. Would the boss have done the same thing if Sita were a white

woman? Contrast the situation to what would have been expected if it had not been an interracial situation (inconsistency).

7. What knowledge does Marisca have about sexual harassment of black women by white men? Use inference from opinions, expectations, knowledge, and other thoughts about racism.

When Marisca told her story, she was not asked to answer all of these questions, but she did provide relevant information with regard to some of them. The account includes a few indications that Marisca has a general knowledge of sexual harassment experienced by women of color. Furthermore, she uses microinformation. As we will see, she refers to forms of discrimination that she has experienced — in a specific manner, in a specific context — so often that she can replay them blindly. Among other things, the experiences of other black people, the behavior of the same person in similar situations, her own experience in similar or different situations, and the opinions of others about the situation are all important.

The Opinions of Others: She declares that there was "terrible gossip" about the boss because he "he couldn't keep his hands off women."

Consistency in the Behavior of the Boss. Marisca asserts that Sita "really" was often "bothered by him." She adds that "in the company, it was a public secret that this man didn't keep his hands to himself and that he always tried it with the darker girls."

Confession by the Person. More often than not there is no confession, but this case was exceptional. The confession of the act (grabbing) as well as the sexual/racial reason for it ("darker girls" attract such attention) came to the fore in the reconstruction of the reaction of the boss to the questions of the branch manager.

Consistency with Experiences of Other Black People. Marisca herself experienced something similar. She says that "last year" she "herself" experienced what Sita "had to deal with"; she also was "grabbed" by a boss, who was also white.

Consistency with Other Situations/Experiences. It should be noted that Marisca mentioned several examples of discrimination in the workplace before she mentioned the story of Sita.

One of Marisca's examples involved the temporary agency K., where she applied with a blond friend from her class, for a position in which knowledge of languages was necessary. First Marisca was told that they only like pastel-colored eye make-up in the company. These are colors that fit a northern European look better than the skin and eye color Marisca has. She suspects that they really want white people and is later supported: Marisca speaks all four languages they ask for and the blond woman only speaks two, but it is she who is called for the job. Beyond this example from the agency, Marisca has encountered some forms of discrimination so often that she anticipates them before they happen. At each new workplace, so she says, her expectations are right on target. She always gets belittling remarks about her "good Dutch" even though she graduated cum laude from a college-prep high school in the Netherlands. This reminds her of her first day as a receptionist at Company E. She says the boss snarled at her that he "doesn't know how *you* [Surinamese] behave, but that *here we* [Dutch people] act differently." This happened at the end of her first day of work, during which Marisca had become so fed up with answering hundreds of telephone calls that she had answered the phone with the name of the company and "How can I help you?" She had left off "Good Afternoon." The boss happened to overhear it. By suggesting that she didn't say "Good Afternoon" because as a Surinamese she did not know about politeness, the boss activated the racial dimension of the situation. This is the shortened and edited version of Marisca's story. In her reconstruction, she used general knowledge of discrimination. She also supported her positions with comparisons to other (similar) situations and experiences. Sexual harassment of a black woman by a white man thus gained meaning through interpretation in terms of other expressions of racism.

I have attempted to illustrate that accounts of racism are not ad hoc narratives. They have their own structure. The method I discussed lends itself not only to the analysis of accounts, but also to the rational inquiry and evaluation of situations in which hidden racism is suspected. The analytical procedure is only a rough framework. Further study can be made, especially in the details of the argumentative structures. It is also important to develop finer methods in order to use memory optimally in the reconstruction of experiences. Finally, my method may form a basis for the development of a normative model for the evaluation of accounts of sexual harassment in a racial context, or, more generally, of racism. Still, truth and trustworthiness are difficult to assess when situations lack a third witness. I hope that my contribution challenges those who automatically assume that blacks who point out racism are overly sensitive. In fact I have identified knowledgeable sensitivity in signaling a problem about which others have remained relatively ignorant and undersensitive.

5
Multiple Identities
On Color and Migration

Identity, Common and Individual

When people share the same history and have the same cultural experience, such as daily habits, language, or religion, and when they start out with the same expectations about the future, the fact of their sharing often shapes a common identity. A feeling of recognition and belonging can develop on the basis of gender, regional, or national origin. The experiences of motherhood or a profession can appeal to a specific identity. We all have multiple identities. Multiple identifications allows us to be flexible in dealing with different people. No matter how different we seem, there is usually some common ground somewhere. This shared identity can be very broad, like being a woman or living in the Netherlands, or very narrow, like having been in the same class or having a friend in common. We are defined by where we come from, but also by what we do as teachers, consultants, salespeople, secretaries, doctors, beauticians, shoemakers, lawyers, hairdressers, or staff members. Various (potential) identities come together in one person. Because of this, I can, with one and the same action of writing, address my self as woman to woman, woman to man, Dutch to Surinamese, Surinamese to Dutch, daughter to mother, professor to student, and person to person.

The subtitle of this chapter, "On Color and Migration," refers to two things: to being a person of color in a white society and to being an

This essay is based on the lecture "Ethnicity and Identity: Women of Surinamese Background in the Netherlands" presented at the Anton de Kom University, Paramaribo, Suriname, 1992.

immigrant. Particular attention will be paid to migration and identity among people from Suriname. Some may have been in the Netherlands since 1960, others since 1980. Others were born and raised in the Netherlands. Each immigrant from Suriname has his or her own migration story, but all also have a story in common. Apart from the indigenous population of Suriname, they are historic immigrants: they are either descendants from the generations who were forced to leave Africa starting more than three hundred years ago, or the children, grandchildren, and great-grandchildren of those who came to Suriname as indentured laborers from India, China, or Indonesia about a hundred years ago. People from Suriname are part of the world history of colonial migration, from one part of the south to another, from the south to the north. The Netherlands became part of Surinamese history a few centuries ago and at the same time, Suriname became part of Dutch history. So Suriname and the Netherlands share a period of history, even though one part of it took place in Suriname and another part in the Netherlands. The Netherlands left an indelible mark on Suriname, and as a result of cultural colonialism, few people from Suriname could escape some degree of Dutch identity.

Most Dutch people of Surinamese background never had a Surinamese nationality because the country was a possession of the kingdom of the Netherlands until 1975. But part of their diverse identity is Surinamese. This part may be broad or very specific, and it may change to some degree or remain unchanged in the Netherlands. At any rate, people from Suriname share part of a common identity and this continues to be the case in the Netherlands.

In Suriname, Surinamese background was not part of one's identity in the same way it is in the Netherlands, where the part that refers to Suriname is shaped in relation to those who are not of Surinamese origin. In Suriname, one was a Surinamese without labeling it, although other parts of identity were named: the African, Indian/Pakistani, Javanese, indigenous, or Chinese origin. There was tolerance, though there was discrimination of light against dark and among ethnic groups. This history is part of the identity of people from Suriname. In the Netherlands, you consciously become "Surinamese," an identity that mixes with earlier identities of African or Asian origin. Some earlier modes of identification become vague, others prominent. Despite the underlying ethnic differences, in a Dutch environment a Surinamese background brings another sort of bond. The earlier color discrimination comes under pressure. Light or dark does not matter so much in the Netherlands: it is clear who isn't white. A person who isn't white is black — a foreigner, an outsider, or an ethnic minority, all terms that signify that the norm is white and European.

Also the identity of Europe is under discussion. Who belongs, who doesn't? Are Europeans naturally white? But people of color have been in Europe for centuries, haven't they? And European culture was shaped by influences from Africa, the Middle East, and Asia, wasn't it? Greek philosophers and scientists were, for example, students of Egyptian teachers. Egyptian culture, in turn, was shaped by influences from southern parts of Africa. But for Europe, its own (read: real) culture historically begins in Greece (Snowden, 1969; Diop, 1974; Mokhtar, 1981).

In former East Germany and Poland, the Vietnamese and Africans who still live there no longer dare to walk on the streets. They get molested. In southern France, North African immigrants are molested and murdered by people belonging to the extreme right. In the United Kingdom, Paki-bashing never lost its appeal for white male youngsters. In Italy, African vendors are subjected to violence on a daily basis. They can be picked out at a glance and marked as non-Europeans, as intruders. Their skin color, the shape of their eyes, the color of their hair, make them stand out. These qualities make them, in the dominant way of thinking, objects of disrespect and aggression. Being persecuted because of skin color or ethnic origin becomes an experience that forms a bond between people, even if they were born thousands of miles apart. It becomes part of one's identity as a person of color or a migrant, although anyone persecuted because of skin color or origin has other distinguishing features, such as originating from an Asian or African background, that further characterize that person. In the Netherlands, being an immigrant of color becomes part of common experience, organization, and action. But at the same time, the other identities remain: the Surinamese part of identity, the Dutch part, the Chinese part.

From Looking Back to Planning the Future

There are several phases in the process of migration that many immigrants from the south probably experience when they come to Europe. The first phase is looking back. At the beginning, there is a rock-solid belief that one will return: the only question is when. A person may live and work in a new place, but the country of origin remains the emotional frame of reference. After about ten years of living away (and, for some people, maybe longer) going back still plays a role, but it becomes less certain. The question no longer is "When are we going back?" but "Are we going back?" The children are in school. The migrant cannot just pick up and leave. It is necessary to deal with the present quite seriously.

Those who look back for too long run the risk of stumbling over things in front of them. At this point the second phase sets in. When one no longer thinks "Well, I'll be going back anyway," it becomes more important to get a good position in this society. Looking back to the country of origin takes on a different meaning: nostalgia, sadness, joy, or solidarity, or, for some people, becomes only a distant memory. The constant comparisons between the Netherlands and the country of origin virtually stop. In their place come the future of the children, career, taking part in special interest groups and representation in political parties. This second phase of looking to the future in the Netherlands marks the start of the awareness of discrimination and racism. For refugees, however, who have seen the ins and outs of the bureaucracy of Fortress Europe, the process of consciousness often proceeds at a much faster pace.

There is a third phase, in which one not only wants to take part in society, but also wants to take some responsibility for the quality of life in the Netherlands. The feeling of "I am in their country and I'll act like they want me to" gives way to "What are my rights and what future do I want for my children?" A certain measure of conformity to the new situation is natural, but fitting in cannot happen unilaterally. Immigrants who finally start feeling Dutch, or who call themselves Dutch, also have a responsibility for Dutch society. This is not only true for the ethnic group they consider themselves part of (other Surinamese, other people of color) but also for society as a whole, and not only for questions of ethnic relations, but also for the environment, disarmament, the neighborhood, or the position of old people. Yet people of color continue to identify with one another in the struggle against racism.

Racism

Racism in the various European countries can differ in the degree of openness about it, but in the end it is all a variation on the same theme:

marginalization, ostracism, and aggression against ethnic groups. This is a structural phenomenon that shows up in the various socioeconomic sectors, such as the labor market, education, and housing. It is also a matter of cultural domination, which is to say one-sided images and exclusion through the media, literature, and communication systems. The degree of racism is determined by the extent to which one's own "kind" and European culture are perceived as naturally better and more developed. The degree of nonracism is determined by the extent of openness to change with a critical perspective vis-à-vis one's own traditions and those of others.

Those who are fighting racism, as individuals or as organizations, take responsibility for the society as a whole. In a society where there is no room for racism, working together with people from different cultural backgrounds is a rich experience. Racism cannot be fought effectively by good intentions alone, because these are usually restricted to the condemnation of openly expressed forms of racism. Intolerance of overt racism, however, can go hand in hand with tolerance of covert forms of racism. This apparent contradiction is supported by the denial that covert discrimination against people of color is embedded in the same power structure from which expressions of overt and blatant racism emerge.

The problem of racism certainly has a moral dimension. Morally and ethically, racism is rejected. But it is not only a question of morals; it is a matter of power relations between the dominant group and other groups, between white citizens — the norm group, the so-called first-class citizens — and the immigrants — the others, the deviants, the so-called second-class citizens. This is the real, symbolic meaning of the concept "Other": not original, second choice, being last to receive provisions such as jobs, education, and housing. In other words, racism maintains a conflict of interests. The process of racism secures the inviolability of the dominant group. The practice of racism regulates who belongs and who does not, who stands in the center and who in the margins. The dominant discourse defines which view or which criticism of the ethnic relationships in the Netherlands is tolerated and which is not; who is allowed to criticize society and who is not; what is acceptable for people of Turkish, Surinamese, Moroccan, or Dutch Antillean origin and what is not. The dominant discourse expresses consensus about what racism is, and what it is not. The monopoly on the definition of racism has led to categorical denial of its existence. Remaining silent in the face of injustices against minorities provides a safe feeling of being within the majority so that it will not turn against one and one won't fall into disfavor. Dissidents and pioneers in progressive movements also risk falling victim:

> The [Dutch] are obsessed with putting down anything that falls outside the accepted norms, rejecting adventure in any form, including adventures of the mind, denying a priori the achievements of those who place themselves above the masses by attracting attention. Woe be to them! Pointed at by hordes of fingers, many give up, give in, compromise, are incapable of a truly rebellious outcry.

This characterization by J. Rentes de Carvalho (quoted in Olink, 1992 [free translation]), Portuguese publicist and commentator on the Dutch character, is an exaggeration, but at the same time, it is close to reality. The majority opinion is increasingly enforced by repressing those voices that do not repeat what others are saying.

Identifying racism as an imbalance of power puts the problem above and beyond the personal level. Still, white citizens often react emotionally and angrily, as if they are personally offended, toward immigrant residents protesting against racism: How dare you tell "us" what is acceptable in "our" country and what is not? How do you dare use the word racism while "we" are a tolerant nation! But doesn't the self-congratulatory idea of being more tolerant (read: better) than the rest of the world lead to a cover for racism? Doesn't the combination of the self-congratulatory attitude and blindness lead to a situation in which opposition against racism is interpreted as an attack on individual freedom of opinion and speech? Isn't it strange that some people become livid when scholars, politicians, and others choose to put the fight against racism high on their list of priorities?

Becoming Aware

The other side of this situation is that people who experience injustice have some responsibility of their own to address the problem. Whoever stands by powerlessly loses self-respect. One can create one's own networks within and outside a neighborhood or workplace. Because, if people cannot defend themselves against the put-downs they experience at work, there will come a time when they actually will feel worthless. *If you let people tamper with your human dignity for too long, you will start to lose faith in your own possibilities and rights as a human being.* I do not want to imply that it is easy to defend oneself or one's group, or that discrimination needs to be solved by people of color alone, but one has to be vigilant. This means becoming aware of one's human rights and the rights of minorities in the Netherlands and in the European Union and it means transmitting this knowledge to children and grandchildren.

In my book *Understanding Everyday Racism* (1991), I discuss the results of a study of two comparable groups of highly educated black women in the United States and the Netherlands. One question I asked them was "What did you, as a girl or as a young woman, learn at home or at school about questions of race relations, ethnic relations, and racism?" Briefly, I found that, the women in the United States, with a few exceptions, were raised to be assertive. They were taught what their ancestors had done against oppression. They learned about power relations between whites and blacks. Parents or other members of the family told stories about the civil rights movement and what black people had achieved. In contrast, only a few Surinamese women had received such information. They were raised with the idea that everything Dutch was good or better, that the Netherlands were a great example of tolerance, and that the people there were nice and rich. No wonder that quite a few people from Suriname took it for granted that people in the Netherlands knew even better what was good for them than they did themselves. And even today, some people are still waiting for the Dutch to take care of them, instead of taking the future in their own hands.

Children Have the Right to Be Proud of Their Heritage

We don't read about it in the newspapers and no one is shouting it from the rooftops, but thousands of Surinamese people in the Netherlands regularly send packages to family and friends in Suriname, containing food and other necessities. I hope that children who are in such families know that this is not a matter of charity, but of commitment, of taking matters into one's own hands, after the Netherlands cut off its development aid to Suriname. It is important to place this commitment in the context of the history of the Surinamese as a people, who are struggling with and trying to liberate themselves from their colonial past. There is a need for liberation from dependence, fear, and powerlessness. This is easily said, but in fact it is a long and painful process. It is absolutely necessary to provide children with cultural self-respect as soon as possible, as is demonstrated by many incidents in schools that are harmful to the self-respect of the children and their parents. What does one do as a black woman, for example, if one's child comes up one day and says "I want a white mother"? Recently a woman told the following story:

> My son Winston told me that he wants a white mother. "Why do you want a white mother?" He thinks they are so nice and, so he says. "And I also want to be white." I think to myself, "Oh God, loekoe sa kon miti mi?!" [Oh God, what is this?] You ask yourself, where is that coming from?! Winston has always been educated by Dutch women at school. Winston is always climbing on Dutch women's laps. How do you deal with that? I mean, do I have to send him to Suriname? But I don't have any friends or family there who are as liberal as I am about raising children. Or rather the ones who feel the same way, don't have children themselves. You see that your child is thinking about the issue of skin color. You talk about Suriname. You tell him "there are only brown people there, people just like you." "There are only brown people there?" the child says. "There are only brown people there, Winston. You never have to get a tan. It is a very nice color and you never look sick." You try to deal with it in your own way. The fact that he is drawn to white women, for instance, is purely because he mainly has white teachers.

This is not a private problem. There are many people from Suriname who can accept some, but not all, aspects of Dutch culture, and who can accept certain, but not all, features of Surinamese culture. There is no internal conflict when one combines within oneself an identity as a Dutch mother, a woman living in Amsterdam who has enlightened ideas about raising children, and an identity as a mother of Surinamese background who is worried that her son may get an overdose of Dutch culture. There is a structural problem, however, namely the lack of teachers of Surinamese, Antillean, Turkish, or Moroccan origin in the education system. Because of this, the children lack recognition of their heritage and find few role models of color to identify with. One teacher of color among many whites is little help because they are often so marginalized that the children and their parents feel that power lies elsewhere, not with the single teacher of color. Parents faced with this situation can be sure that other children of color are also coming home with such stories. It is important not to deal with this alone. Speaking to other parents can open up possibilities of working together to give the children enough positive identification in school. This requires co-operation between parents of Surinamese, Turkish, Moroccan, and other backgrounds, as well as white Dutch parents who think it is important for their children to have a positive role model in parents and teachers of color.

Another Surinamese mother saw a very cute white boy standing at her door, asking for "Hans." "But there is no 'Hans' here," said the mother, who does have a son by the name of Ricardo. "But," said the boy at the door, "yesterday I dropped Hans off here and I was supposed to pick him up again today." Later, it turns out that Ricardo used the name "Hans" at school, in the hope that he would not be seen as "different."

Situations like this demand action, but what one can do depends on the relationship a parent has with her child and the support available from others. There are no guidelines for a proper response, but it is also not an individual problem. The denial or shame about color or ethnicity is the everyday reality with which parents of color in a white society have to deal.

Children who are well informed by their parents about racism and discrimination do not run as high a risk of having identity problems (Wilson, 1987; Tizard & Phoenix, 1993). Providing information may not prevent discrimination, but by doing so, parents of color give a clear message to the child: "Our position is not the way we want it to be. Discrimination is not fun, it is not right, but we do something about it whenever we can." To decide to protect children by not telling them anything for fear of spoiling their carefree thoughts is not necessarily the right choice. Such a decision is more likely to create confusion. Children are not completely innocent. Those who hear from their parents that there is equal opportunity for all, yet at the same time sense that they are not treated fairly in school, get confused. Informing children about injustice must go hand in hand with creating a positive attitude about what one can accomplish as a group, despite discrimination. Feedback from others on this issue is important, but the question is: How does one organize support, how does one receive support from others? How does one become assertive, as a woman of color, as a man of color, as an ethnic minority group?

Assertiveness against Racism

A prerequisite for assertiveness is recognizing and understanding the mechanisms and politics of racism. Recognition of racism involves anger, but it is important to be able to put anger aside in order to make a strategic plan. It is not a good idea to get stuck in complaining about how horrible things are. Crying clears the air, but it does little to help in the long run. An attitude of "cleaning up the mess" and "dealing with the issue" will be far more effective. In other words, an assertive attitude is essential.

Assertiveness is usually associated with psychological characteristics such as courage and self-confidence. I will use the term in a broader sense. Assertiveness can have social, economic, political, cultural, and psychological dimensions. *Social assertiveness* by my definition is knowledge of the society in which one lives, of its institutions and its networks. It also includes the ability to set up new networks for personal or group purposes. *Economic assertiveness* is the decision to invest in the means and talents of one's community with the goal of improving technical, professional, analytic, and communicative skills and of expanding the financial power of the group. *Political assertiveness* means recognizing relevant channels and using them to protect group and individual civil rights. *Cultural assertiveness* is the capacity to expand one's possibilities by using key elements of the norms, values, communicative and other culturally specific skills with which one grew up. *Psychological assertiveness* is the ability to value elements in the dominant culture without loss of self-esteem and is expressed in self-confidence. It is knowing how to use the valuable elements of one's own culture without rejecting everything Dutch out of a misdirected longing for one's own traditions. It involves taking a critical position on those elements in cultures that stand in the way of respecting all people and valuing diversity. In conclusion, assertiveness requires a critical view on culture and traditions. It requires self-respect, social power, and economic resilience — despite racism.

6

How Positive Is "Positive Action"?

We are sitting on stage at a long table, looking out at a room filled with about five hundred people. We are at a forum on education and the workplace. The occasion is the tenth anniversary of an organization for people from ethnic minority groups. To my left there is a representative of an employers' association, a man. He is the first respondent to a paper about causes of unemployment among ethnic minorities. He keeps it short. Everyone can agree with his view stressing the importance of good education and perseverance in order to obtain a position on the job market. "Employers," he triumphantly concludes, "would like to hire qualified ethnic minorities, but they should be able to find them!"

"Then you must have overlooked the studies showing that more than half of the employers want qualified applicants, but would rather take white Dutch people. And you must have overlooked all the highly educated Antilleans and Surinamese who can't find a job!" The trade union woman, sitting on my right, jumps right in. "Don't make me laugh. Employers can say all these wonderful things," she continues her argument, "but when it comes down to it, they don't even reach the lowest targets for hiring women and ethnic minorities." "So you are in favor of positive action?" the chair of the forum, a man, recapitulates. [as explained in the introduction, positive action resembles affirmative action — trans.] While the union woman to my right says "Yes, of course, the trade union has taken a very clear position on that matter," I feel the male employer to my left shake his head as if to say "no" and mumble something inaudible.

The usual back and forth has started. I don't like it very much. Polarization grows, leaving no room to modify or revise the positions taken. Preventing loss of face becomes more important than addressing the problem of unemployment. They dig themselves in and hear only what the other party says against their point of view. Whoever wins support from a third party wins the point. "And you, Dr. Essed?" all attention is suddenly focused on me. "Are you for or against positive action?" The chair looks at me expectantly. "Well, on the one hand," I begin. "No, not 'on the one hand, on the other hand,'" he interrupts me, falling into a pattern that often occurs in discussions of positive action, where an atmosphere is created in which the views are diametrically opposed. There is no room for reflection, no room for "yes, provided there is . . ." or "no, unless we see. . . ." Dissecting positive action was not on the agenda of that forum. I will use this chapter to explore the question "How positive is positive action?"

Positive action is a controversial subject. It is a sensitive issue and there are many misunderstandings about it. For a while, positive action was a popular topic of discussion. For this reason, I didn't want to address it publicly until now. Words are quickly twisted and misused when the topic is a trendy one. Many people, or so it appears when I mention positive action, automatically translate my critical stance toward racism into a stance in favor of positive action. But I have never been a champion of so-called positive action. Taking a public stand on the issue, however, is a precarious matter. If you say you are for it, you recognize the problem of structural discrimination in the workplace, against women and ethnic groups. After all, the aim of positive action is to correct the inequality caused by discrimination. So far, so good. But what guarantees are there that discrimination will be counteracted by positive action? What makes me angry is the arrogance with which the carrot of positive action is held up to women of various backgrounds in the front parlor, while negative action continues in the back parlor with "business as usual." On top of the already existing prejudice that women and people of color are less competent, we get a new version based on positive action pouring old prejudices into new bottles: "people who were hired through positive action were probably not competent enough to get in on their own strength."

Positive action does not necessarily have a positive effect. However, if you take a stand against it, you are back to square one. You find yourself on the side of those who feel all this talk about discrimination is nonsense. They assume somewhat naively that only the "best" candidate gets hired anyway. "Or did you want to discriminate against white men?" Of course, you can explain that the "objective" choice of the "best" candidate is a myth. Many institutions and companies would certainly function better if they had indeed hired the best candidates. However, studies have shown that the choice often automatically goes in favor of the white male candidate, even if there were candidates of Surinamese, Antillean, or Turkish heritage with better qualifications (den Uyl, Choenni, & Bovenkerk, 1986; Willemsen, 1988; Verhaar, 1991). And even among the white men, the best qualified are not always hired, because there is no such thing as objective selection. One can speak for hours or write whole books coming up with arguments for and against *positive* action — just like a Ping-Pong game. I personally never really liked Ping-Pong debates because they are win or lose situations; they blind you to options that lie beyond the Ping-Pong table. I hope to point to another course of action in this chapter. I will discuss several side effects of positive action which show up in practice. I will reduce the idea of positive action to its true proportions. It is an instrument, not a goal in itself. The questions I ask are: What kind of vision of society does positive action fit into? What diagnosis can propose positive action as a solution? Is the diagnosis correct? And are the negative side effects of positive action inherent in positive action (Kempadoo, 1988)?

Positive action has different implications for white women and women of color. The first group is excluded on the basis of gender discrimination, the second, on the basis of gender and race/ethnic discrimination (Meulenbelt, 1985; Essed, 1991; Lutz, 1991). I will not go into the differences so much because there are enough similarities, certainly as far as the assumptions underlying positive action are concerned.

A Society That Labels the Majority a Problem

Positive action exists in as many versions as there are companies claiming to implement the policy. In most cases, the policy derails right from the point where positive action is seen as the answer to the so-called problem groups on the job market. A while ago I saw the whole list again, one group after the other: women, ethnic minorities, the disabled, homosexuals, and older people. I looked at the list and thought to myself — what are they saying here? Women are a problem? Okay, that makes half the population unproblematic, men. But minorities also seem to be a problem. That leaves white men of Dutch origin. And disabled people are also a problem? Aha! That leaves the able-bodied white men of Dutch origin. But older people and homosexuals are also considered problem groups. So the only people left are relatively young, able-bodied, white straight men of Dutch origin.

What kind of society is this, in which everyone is considered a problem, except for a group that is numerically a minority: male, not old, heterosexual, of Dutch origin, and, of course, white — ? I do not want to imply that every white man is better off, or that there are no successful women and people of color, but it does seem as though the job market is arranged so that the qualifications "white" (Western European), younger, able-bodied, male, heterosexual are automatically advantageous, and that the rest, which basically means the overwhelming majority, are automatically a problem.

The concept of positive action is misleading, because it suggests that there was never any action in favor of any group before. Now, all of a sudden, it is an issue concerning women as a group, and men and women of color. It is not often stated this way, but many companies would not have remained dominated by white males for so long if there had not been an unquestioned, traditional preference for employees who fit the profile. And this situation regenerates itself. There is no real tendency to doubt whether men are the best workers and managers.

The Myth of Objective Selection Criteria

Various organizations claim to implement a policy of positive action for women and ethnic minorities. There are three possible variations in positive action where it concerns personnel treatment (De Jong & Verkuyten, 1990). In the weakest type, people from ethnic minorities are given preference in cases of equal competence. (I will get back to the impossibility of "equal competence.") In a stronger form of positive action, people from target groups are given priority if they show the required competence. In the most radical variation, representatives of the target groups are given preference regardless of their qualifications.

The first problem occurs in the job ads. One often reads: "In cases of sufficient competence, we will give preference to a woman"; or, "In cases of equal competence, we will give preference to candidates from ethnic minority groups." I ask myself how women of Surinamese, Turkish, or Moroccan origin should apply. If they are looking for an employee of color they might prefer a man, or if they are looking for a woman they probably prefer a white woman. In either case you might as well forget it. In other words, even at the application stage, the idea of preference begins to look shaky.

A second problem is the suggestion that there is such a thing as equal competence. Social, normative criteria such as motivation, reliability, flexibility, and fit cannot be measured objectively, but often they play a bigger role in hiring and promotion of employees than hard facts such as degrees and diplomas. Even degrees become subjective when one asks — as is increasingly the case — for an "academic level of thinking" instead of a university or college degree. The most one can say is that candidates have qualities and traits that the organization appreciates.

The third problem concerns the policy of having a target group. Positive action programs assume that women and ethnic minority groups are at a disadvantage relative to Dutch men, so that means they have a problem. Positive action policies are an attempt by the government to convince employers to attract employees from the target groups. "How do you attract them and how do you keep them?" reads the slogan by the policymakers. Almost unnoticeably, the attention shifts from discrimination by the employers to the groups that experience discrimination. An image is created that they don't want to or don't know how to find a job. They not only have a problem, they also become a problem for others, who are now required to make the effort to attract people from those groups. It is not surprising then that many employers feel strengthened in the existing belief that letting in women and ethnic minorities means letting in problems. And, the employer continues this train of thought, by letting in problems, you risk getting problems yourself.

This last point brings up a deeper question: What exactly do we mean by the term "quality"? If the definition is only (unconsciously) inspired by what white men have to offer, it would seem to me limited by definition. Seeking optimal quality certainly isn't the issue then. The unquestioned preference for Western Europeans and males works to the advantage of candidates who fit that profile. If we do not start by critically questioning this profile, there is a chance that a positive action will result in tolerating a certain number of "deviant" (read: less right for the job, since right meets the traditional profile) workers. Why not, for instance, include the requirement in the profile of managers that they have significant experience with diverse populations. And, as far as I am concerned, knowledge and experience with antidiscrimination interventions and human resource management would also be an asset. And there are many more creative and sensible ideas for management to consider (Essed & Helwig, 1992; see also Chapter 7 below). Unfortunately, we have not come that far yet.

A policy of positive action does not change the fact that employers initially weigh the qualities of individual women and people of color against two grids: the normative views on the white man and existing ethnic and gender stereotypes (Pettigrew & Martin, 1989). In other words, women or candidates of color, do not only compete with other applicants; they must also prove themselves in light of a dominant negative group image! Assertive women are immediately seen as unfeminine and aggressive, but people who cannot act decisively get passed over for management track jobs! In the evaluators' perception warning lights start flashing when they get female candidates of Muslim background: "language deficiency" or "their husbands won't allow them to work" (Arends, 1990). In case of refugees the alarm goes off: "can't fit in" and "have to deal with them differently." On the issue of the new employees fitting in, the fire brigade is called in: "one Turkish woman among Dutch people is asking for trouble."

Once again, the discussion of positive action obscures the fact that there has always been action in favor of white men. Take the following examples:

1. An academic position is advertised worldwide. The top group of applicants includes national and international scholars, male and female. The outstanding candidate is a woman of Dutch origin. She has written many books and leaves the other candidates miles behind when it comes to international reputation. When there is no way around seriously considering her, the rumors start. "Difficult person." "Taking her means the end of peace and quiet in your department." They range from bad to worse. "She sleeps around with everybody." But what does her sex life have to do with her knowledge and ability as a scholar? And since when is the professional competence of men measured by their sex lives? She finally does get the job. She is slightly battered because at this point there has even been speculation about "who she has done 'it' with." An offer is extended and she turns out to be a brilliant and dynamic addition to the institute.

2. An academic position is advertised worldwide. As in most specializations, there are also a few top names in the field. And bingo, one of those top people applies! And guess what, she is a woman! And, believe

it or not, she is from a Third World country! Besides the impressive number of books she has written, she has also received various prizes and honorary doctorates. Before the interview begins, a rumor circulates that she is "aggressive." The interview with the selection committee, consisting entirely of white men, becomes an embarrassing spectacle. One of them asks if she has any experience in teaching classes and remarks that teaching is serious business in Holland. Another tries to find out if she knows the relevant theories in her field of specialization. Shortly after the encounter with this committee, she withdraws her application. She is furious. She has never been so insulted in her life. Moreover, one of the committee members would have been a future colleague. She would not work with someone like that for a million dollars. The position is subsequently given to a European man of fairly obscure reputation.

3. An academic position is not advertised. The job is offered to a Dutch man. There are no rumors about his sex life, nor about his personal character, nor about how his qualities compare to any other candidates, who, in any case, were never given the opportunity to apply.

In each of these examples, the positive action policy toward women was in place. If we make up the balance, it turns out to be overwhelmingly in favor of men: the woman from the first example, who stood out way above the other candidates, might also have been confronted with opposition and smear campaigns before she got the job if no positive action had existed. Positive action policy just added more fuel to the fire. Her performance will be questioned whenever that is expedient, in the light of the stigma of having been hired under the positive action policy toward women.

The unknown man of the second example — who got the job because the better female candidate was insulted to the point that she withdrew — gets more than he deserves. Because nothing stays hidden in a small country like the Netherlands, it becomes a public secret that there was another "top" candidate. But now he got the job, so imagine how good he must be. . . .

In the third example, only one man got a chance at the job. He did not have to compete with others. On top of that, he gets a lot of honor and praise. He gets an ego boost from the notion that people thought he was so right for the job that the application procedure was seen as a waste of money and energy.

Examples such as these are not unique (Verhaar, 1991). Of course, some, or maybe many, women get the jobs they are looking for without any problems under the protection of positive action. However, there is always the question to what extent they got their jobs due to positive action? Or worse, can we be sure that they would not have been hired if there had not been a positive action policy?

Exclusion Mechanisms

I have already mentioned that positive action fits a pattern of thinking that assumes the disadvantaged position of the target groups. It is not the organization that is questioned, but rather the target groups themselves. They are assumed incapable of entering the job market on their own merit. In practice, positive action is usually a matter of quantitative measurements increasing the number of women and representatives of ethnic groups at various levels in the job market, and not so much a matter of the qualitative aspects. Qualitative aspects have to do with working conditions and career opportunities for each employee. A prerequisite to that is a work atmosphere free of discrimination where personal qualities are recognized and stimulated and are allowed to develop to the maximum benefit of the organization. This is more than just taking a course here and there. It is a matter of a change in company culture. I will come back to company cultural change later.

The practice of positive action does not go much further than allowing women and ethnic groups to get a foot in the door. Those who do get in land in a relatively homogeneous corporate culture where the norm is male and Dutch. There is little or no room for cultural diversity. One of the weakest links in the idea of positive action is the lack of awareness of the importance of the quality of the corporate culture and the atmosphere between employees of various backgrounds. This is not surprising because positive action deals with making up for disadvantages relative to the (white) male norm. The norm itself remains unquestioned and positive. This process is already evident in the selection process and often also shows up in the workplace itself. Therefore I will discuss several mechanisms which can turn up.

Ethnization of the Work

"Ethnization" refers to the development of ethnic clusters and dimensions in the job market. Group interests and employment increasingly run along ethnic lines, whereby people of color stay in the margins, while white people remain in the center of the political and economic stage. Ethnization also shows up in the language where we have become familiar with terms like ethnic work, ethnic clients, ethnic studies, and ethnic educational tracks in ethnic departments. Ethnization is institutionalized in practice, where the work of various groups runs along separate lines. Thereby Turks should preferably work for Turks and Surinamese for Surinamese. Native Dutch people take on the role of "objective" regulators and decision makers as if only they are able to work with everyone—their own as well as other ethnic groups. This process of specification and selection reproduces itself. Women of color—even at the managerial levels—are geared to ethnic work directed at their own group. This is especially true for the service sectors.

The following example shows how ethnization of the workplace can happen in practice. It concerns a health consultant of Surinamese origin, the only woman of color among an all-white staff. We will call her Joanne Guda. Joanne has gotten more and more ethnic clients in her caseload over the last few years, while white clients are taken care of by white colleagues. She has mixed feelings about this, because she wasn't hired to work with ethnic clients only. In a way, however, she feels morally obliged to help the ethnic clients as much as possible, in a large part because she is much more comfortable in dealing with their situation than her white colleagues are.

Joanne was educated in the Netherlands, just like her white colleagues. She has all the qualifications to work with Dutch clients, or with any clients for that matter, but she has an advantage over her colleagues in that her Surinamese background gives her greater experience in dealing with people of different cultural backgrounds. She can also more readily deal with the psychological (and possibly psychosomatic) problems ethnic clients experience because of their exposure to hostility, rejection, and discrimination in society. Because of this extra knowledge and ability, she slowly but surely becomes the specialist on ethnic clients.

Initially, Joanne's clients were mostly from Suriname, the Antilles, and Aruba, but lately, she also has the Moroccan and Turkish clients. She sees this as an interesting development and requests some additional training to help these groups better. The request is denied because the management feels that a Surinamese woman cannot work with Turkish or Moroccan clients. Shortly afterward a white Dutch colleague is transferred into her department to work with the Turkish and Moroccan clients. Before the transfer, the white colleague takes the courses the Surinamese woman had wanted to take. The courses are financed out of the institution's "ethnic fund."

Unrealistic Expectations

Organizations often have unrealistic expectations regarding women from ethnic groups. This is certainly true when their arrival is announced with the trumpet sounds of positive action. This, incidentally, also often happens with women of white Dutch origin and men from ethnic minority backgrounds. One is perceived as either fantastic or a total klutz and one's performance is measured accordingly. It quickly turns out that the newcomer is seen as the ambassador for all other ethnic groups or all other women.

Given the inequality in power and the role of prejudice, there is a disproportionate pressure on the newly hired woman not to make mistakes. Each mistake can reinforce stereotypes about her unsuitability: "See, I told you so!" This can also be a self-fulfilling prophecy. Anyone who has to be on her toes constantly will feel the pressure and start making mistakes. Women often internalize the expectation that they have to perform exceptionally well and the fear of failure that comes with it. This makes it even more difficult to break through the mechanism of exaggerated expectations.

Major Assessment Errors

This mechanism has to do with the previous point because white colleagues are often not capable of judging the performance of women of color without applying their prejudices about ethnic minorities. Again, there are similarities in the way white Dutch women and men from ethnic groups are assessed. Good job performances by Moroccan, Surinamese, or other ethnic minority women seem to have very little effect on general ideas about these groups. The perception that people of color are less able remains in effect and the qualities of one coworker of color are interpreted as an exception to the rule. Poor performance by ethnic women, however, serves as proof that ethnic employees in general are less competent. As a result they run the risk of not being able to trust comments about their work. Do they take compliments with a grain of salt because they know they are judged on the usual low expectations of other ethnic women? Or should they take harsh criticism with a grain of salt because it can be an expression of prejudice against people of color, at least in part?

No Top Jobs

In addition to evaluations of coworkers of color being influenced by prejudice, there is the issue of real exclusion. One example comes from a librarian of Moluccan descent. We will call her Rena Telohy. She works in a library with various branches. She has always hoped to be transferred to the Information Services Coordination department, a popular position because the library offers few other career opportunities. At first she was told that her qualifications were insufficient, so she decided to do something about it and took the necessary evening courses to qualify. About four years later, there was a vacancy in the Coordination Department. The head of the department, a man, approached Rena and said that she was the only employee with the required qualifications and that "they have no other option but to hire her." But would she please be willing to wait for the job a little longer, because it would be a good opportunity for the department to get someone from outside? Rena lets herself be intimidated. This "vote of confidence" by the head of her department spells nothing but trouble for the years ahead if she doesn't give in. Then this head left and by that time the institution has implemented the policy of positive action.

Luckily for Rena, there is another vacancy in the Coordination Department. Rena finally gets the job she has wanted for so long, but now the story goes that she got the job because of her color, and that she had to be promoted because of positive action. It is rumored that she did not get the position on her own merit. The difference with the situation earlier is that at first she was passed over because of the prejudice that a woman of color does not belong in that kind of job. Now she has the job, but people still feel a person of color doesn't really belong there and that she should not have been given the job. The prejudice has not changed. She has the job, but now she has to deal with subordinates questioning her authority before she has even started. It will take a disproportionate personal effort by Rena to keep from becoming so irritated that she wants to leave. Without intervention we may see a common pattern develop where subordinates sabotage her orders, criticize her every move, and start complaining about her whenever they get a chance.

Inclusion Mechanisms

The stigma of having been hired not because one is good, but because one is a woman or a member of an ethnic minority does not make life any easier. It neatly fits into the existing gender and ethnic prejudices. Of course, the solution does not lie in more exclusion (we may as well forget about hiring women or people of color) but in developing mechanisms of inclusion wherein the presence of women and people of different ethnic backgrounds is not associated with problems.

It is possible to do things differently. In the above case, it would help if the new department head, a woman, made sure there is no misunderstanding about Rena's having gotten this job because of her long experience in the institution and because of her ability. The department head can talk about the many younger coworkers who have already been trained under Rena's guidance, about her being more than qualified for this well-earned promotion, about many things. This kind of introduction to the colleagues would make it clear that the organization, including the top management, stands behind the promotion. If introductions are not part of the corporate culture (which seems a serious flaw in the organization to me), then there are certainly other ways to shed a positive light on Rena's appointment.

Another example takes place in a supermarket, which has no policy of positive action. It is hard to get people to work in this sector, and there is a shortage of personnel. If the personnel manager were asked whom he would prefer among equal candidates — a young white man or a young ethnic woman — he cries "What do you mean, choose? Are you suggesting I would let a suitable candidate get away? These times you take both!" So both are hired. The young woman, Turkish background, is very nice, polite, helpful to the customers, and actually a good example of a positive worker at the cash register. However, the situation couldn't have been more stereotypical: she covers her head with a scarf, a sign of tradition. Some customers avoid her register, some are aggressive. The manager could react to this by saying: "I will not hire her after the probation period. She just doesn't fit into our corporate culture." By doing this, he would stigmatize the friendly cashier, who does her work outstandingly — head scarf and all.

Instead, he confronts the aggressive customers, who make insulting remarks about Islam. One even deliberately throws the money on the floor instead of handing it to the cashier. The manager's response is straightforward: people who can't treat our cashier in a decent manner can go and shop somewhere else. This is a clear signal to the customers, but also clear feedback for his cashier. He implicitly lets her know "we are happy with you and if a customer isn't happy with you, we aren't happy with that customer." The manager goes one step further: during the job interview he had noticed that this young woman had a lot of potential. He decides to put her in a training course, so that she can move up to a better position earlier than he had originally planned. The manager is thinking ahead: If this Turkish woman gets a higher position, maybe that will attract more Turkish employees, or other ethnic employees and more ethnic customers. And everybody will just simply get used to it.

This is creative management. The manager does not accept that his employee is a problem because he has the confidence to take decisive steps against discrimination. The problem, as he sees it, are the people who are unwilling to see her competence and friendliness because of her ethnic background. It is not surprising that this manager also sees the other qualities in his worker, enabling her to get a better position in the supermarket and putting her skills to better use.

Just Deal with Discrimination

If only things always turned out so nicely! At this point, I come to the lack of knowledge and the feeling of powerlessness many managers have in adequately recognizing and dealing with discrimination. I don't mean to imply that discrimination especially or specifically concerns hostile interactions on the shop floor that frequently isolate workers of color from the team. The shop floor becomes or remains an arena where exclusion takes place, partly because managers do not succeed in showing that they won't tolerate discrimination. Many organizations could benefit from adding new aspects to the requirements for good management: the idea that managers ought to be able to lead culturally diverse teams and know how to deal effectively with discrimination.

Another problem concerns the distinction between the qualities an employee may have as an individual and qualities that may come from a given sociocultural background. Unfortunately noticing differences as such is sometimes perceived as a form of discrimination. However, acknowledging differences is not a problem in itself. The problem is the mechanism with which such differences are hierarchically structured. If one automatically—which is to say without thinking about it— associates dark skin color, or Turkish or Antillean background with "inferior" and potential problems, the very mention of difference becomes threatening, because difference will trigger hierarchical thinking. The solution to this dilemma is not to deny that one makes these differences or to pretend color blindness, because that is simply impossible. Sometimes it is relevant to acknowledge a difference, which is not the same as being a racist. Racism involves differentiation in cases when making a difference is not at all relevant. Many people do not understand that they can simply get information about what racism is, what discrimination is, and when it is important to recognize differences. Instead these people take on the martyr role: "We can't say anything anymore. If you say 'Turk,' you are already called a racist."

It is narrow-minded to divide people into racists and antiracists, as if one group does nothing but discriminate and the other does nothing but fight discrimination. Sometimes there is discrimination and sometimes there is no discrimination. We are talking about practices involving one person and not another, involving some persons more than others, and involving some situations and not others. For example: the head librarian mentioned above, who automatically lacked trust in the qualities of Rena, may have an angry discussion with his neighbor who wants Turks and Moroccans "to get the hell out of the country." Reality is more complex than dividing people up into racists and nonracists or racists and antiracists. People certainly play an essential role in continuing racism by their practices, but fighting people is not the solution. You can fight what people do: publicly voicing racist ideas, spreading prejudice through the media, verbally attacking ethnic groups, discriminating in employments, excluding and marginalizing ethnic groups in sectors of society.

Opting for Diversity

Back to the question of how positive "positive action" is. I purposely did not discuss whether I am "for" or "against" it because that would have created the illusion that positive action is the only choice. It is like someone who has been kept hungry for years and who is then promised a truckload of bread and butter; for free, every day, for the next few years, but only bread and butter. If you say yes, you won't be hungry for the next few years, but what you have chosen isn't really healthy either. If you say no, you may never get rid of your hunger.

I make a different choice. First of all, I advocate another point of departure: no half-hearted measures to combat the so-called disadvantages, but granting the right to work and acknowledging respect for human qualities. I choose an approach in which room for diversity is central. I often work in culturally mixed teams that include different professions, genders, ethnicities, and ages. Sometimes this choice has a few drawbacks. It can take a little more time to establish efficient communication. The advantages of working with culturally mixed teams, however, far outweigh the disadvantages, because diversity in options and points of view will make a better product and, in the long run, a better working environment.

Appreciating diversity means breaking through the mechanism with which the idea of "we" (native whites, men) are associated with "positive" qualities (they are rational, trustworthy, civilized, motivated) whereas the notion of "they" (people of color, women) is associated with "negative" characteristics, or qualities of inferior status (they are emotional, incompetent, unprofessional, unambitious).

Accommodating diversity is a challenge to corporate culture, as well as to the cultural backgrounds of everyone involved to test how useful their own assumptions are for the labor market of the year 2000 and beyond. The choice in favor of quality and the diverse and unique talents and needs of employees often leads to constructive changes in the culture of the organization, as can be seen in the following example.

Company A in Amsterdam wants to update its services and get in tune with the 1990s, which implies hiring more people of color. At first, things don't go as smoothly as they had hoped. A closer study reveals problems with the selection criteria, which are apparently Eurocentric. So the managers take some training in quality selection, focusing not only on criteria that might have a negative ethnic effect, but also on criteria that may be discriminatory in terms of gender. This focus on the effective evaluation of employee qualifications also makes it possible to discuss another problem with hiring and promoting staff: existing co-optation practices. There had been growing discontent among the (still predominantly white male) employees about the arbitrary nature and nepotism of promotions, but no one dared to raise the issue for fear of repercussions. Now they take the opportunity to say something about it. In short, after raising matters that seemed to pertain only to hiring ethnic staff, there are now effects with wider applications: the management quality is improved by improving the selection criteria and promotion procedures.

In sum: my argument is not for or against positive action, but rather for a policy that corrects discrimination and puts unambiguous sanctions in place. This means creating user friendly antidiscrimination guidelines. There will certainly still be organizations that need further incentives before they start hiring women and people from ethnic groups. Maybe they will eventually adopt positive action under pressure from the government. There might be a visible numerical change, but the quality of the working environment may leave much to be desired. The white Dutch male worker will probably keep a privileged position, especially at the higher management levels. Maybe we have to say "better some bread and butter than no food at all" as far as these organizations are concerned.

Apart from applying pressure and sanctions, positive developments can also be stimulated and rewarded. Many employers will only be convinced when they see positive results from others. This is why I argue for investment in diversity development (see Chapter 7) and in the development of models for managing diversity representing relatively new directions in organizational development, in the Netherlands as well as abroad (ISIS, 1992; Hunter, Kaufman & Davis, 1995; Essed, in press). The government can stimulate this innovation through research, by subsidizing test situations, training, or incentives, by providing information, and so on. A growing number of organizations recognize that human resources are too valuable to leave underutilized. They are discovering the advantages of working toward a common goal with men and women with different cultural backgrounds, expertise, and experience. They appreciate the range of cultural influences in (Western) Europe, because they know that managing diversity is the reality of today and tomorrow.

Making room for diversity in the workplace means opting for an inclusive working atmosphere. It means taking a firm stand, without doubt or fear, against racism and discrimination within the organization. More and more employers are discovering that a diverse climate improves the quality of work and the working situation. They have invested in the consulting services or training required for its implementation within the management structure and within the work sphere, and they are beginning to reap the benefits (Morrison, Ruderman, & Hughes-James, 1993). Because they have opted for ethnic and gender diversity in their goals and policies, they do not need positive action. Their actions have already proved to be positive.

7

Encouraging Diversity in Colleges and Universities

A Microlevel Sketch

A new colleague is moving into the office I already share with someone else, and it isn't a terribly large office to begin with. Moving around the desks and bookcases, we start to get a feeling for each other's tastes, discussing the various possibilities, laughing about little things, in short, everything we do is also a search for a balance in our interactions based on respect for each other. To my surprise, the new setup in the office is pretty nice. Still, my other colleague and I didn't think anything was wrong with the office before. The arrival of the new colleague created a good opportunity to take a critical look at the objects in the room. A few things could be thrown out, because they were not as useful as we had hoped. The third colleague also suggested some new things that had come in handy in her last job. In the new arrangement, we have less space to walk but we each have our own spot where we feel at home.

This moving-in ritual fascinated me. While thinking about it, I saw an analogy to another issue: namely the integration of ethnic minorities. Usually, minorities get the message that it is a favor to join so it is their job to fit in. But how different things would have looked for our new colleague if her only choice had been to take the single spot that happened to be free — probably the least attractive spot otherwise we would have already claimed it. This might also have created an atmosphere of "first come, first served" which automatically turns those who arrived later into a problem: "as long as she doesn't do this or that, because then we can no longer do such and such." That kind of climate is not conducive to making useful suggestions, which the organization as a whole might profit from.

In short, when the new worker arrived the primary focus was not "how do we fit her in?" but "how do we create a new balance by changing along as well?" This is still not an ideal situation, but it is a good basis for working together. The new colleague brings new expertise to the organization, new views, and—with them—new possibilities. These advantages amply outweigh the space we lost, the need to now share a telephone with a third person, and the necessity of making arrangements about scheduling appointments and receiving visitors.

A Macrolevel Sketch

The population of various large cities in the Netherlands has changed dramatically in the last twenty years. In Amsterdam, for example, more than 25 percent of the people come from the south or have parents from there: Suriname, the Netherlands Antilles, Aruba, Turkey, Morocco, Ghana, Pakistan, China, and elsewhere. In the year 2010, their number may have increased to 50 percent. The ethnic face of the schools in Amsterdam has also changed. The average Amsterdam school is no longer totally white but is now multiethnic. Half of the children have parents who came from the south. This type of change can also be seen in the job market.

The trend toward a multiethnic labor force is also apparent in places other than the Netherlands. Similar developments are taking place elsewhere. The forecast for the United States is that 29 percent of the people who enter the job market will be from ethnic minorities by the year 2000 and that more than 60 percent of all women of working age will be part of the labor force (Sekaran & Leong, 1992b). In the United States, the demand by organizations for new research data and policy proposals to trace and fight gender and ethnic exclusion grew in the 1980s (Fernandez, 1981; Morrison, White, Van Velsor, & Center for Creative Leadership, 1987). Heading toward Work Force 2000 — the potential for the year 2000 — more and more organizations are using the diversity in the labor supply to their advantage. They invest in diversity training courses, consultants, and development of the leadership of the future: managers for organizations with workers from different backgrounds (Fernandez, 1991; Morrison, 1992; Sekaran & Leong, 1992a; Thomas, 1991; van der Werf, 1992; AIMD, 1996).

Teaching Future Managers and Leaders

The media regularly pays attention to ethnic relations in elementary and high schools. Terms such as intercultural education, bilingual classes, and "white" and "black" schools are now widely used. So far, issues of ethnic diversity do not play as much in European colleges and universities. Still, it is important to see what changes might be desirable in these institutions, where, after all, the middle and top managers of the future are being educated.

In this rather practical chapter, I will make suggestions as to how to stay in touch with the reality that greater numbers of students and teachers from ethnic minorities are getting into higher education. I do not intend to outline a scenario of what to do, but I will identify some key factors in a process of change. One has to keep in mind that blueprints usually do not work, because changes develop gradually over time and according to the specific context.

Managing a diverse workplace helps broaden one's perspective. Colleges and universities anticipating diversifying the work force adapt their courses and offer training in the skills and know-how deemed necessary for future managers, personnel officers, supervisors, policymakers, engineers, doctors, social workers, and others who will work in culturally mixed teams. This is not to say that the idea of diversity or heterogeneity is new. We are all familiar with variety within professions and between positions and tasks in the workplace. Nobody would put her child in a school where they teach geography, but no arithmetic, language, or history. A healthy diet is one with a variety of minerals and vitamins. Consumers appreciate variety in the choice of the products they are offered. In the same way, organizations with a diverse staff have access to a broader range of relevant insights and perspectives on specific assignments than are available in homogeneous environments. In other words, welcoming diversity becomes a new source of competitive advantage.

Diversity may also mean that the quality of courses will improve; Eurocentric material can be replaced, and the teaching staff will become more varied. In developing a climate for diversity we will be challenged to be creative and innovative. Moreover, in a rapidly changing world, it is imperative that organizations constantly question underlying assumptions in order to keep improving the quality of their product. Exposure to diversity may show that habits and customs that were taken for granted, both by the dominant majority and by ethnic minorities, are not universal. Diversity facilitates the open discussion of opposing points of view, promoting the recognition of different standards and the search for new ideas (Kouzes and Posner, 1993). The goal is that organizations will not state "this is how we are used to doing it," but will instead consider "even though this is how we are used to doing it, is that how we really want to do it, and why? What do we want to keep as is, and what do we want to do differently, and better? What does it take to create more variety in resources and talents to extend our capacity?" An organization posing these kinds of questions may be ready to accommodate diversity.

Preconditions for Development of Diversity

Diversity in the workplace, a transformational development, works only for those organizations that give sufficient priority to their human resource management (Tichy & Devanna, 1986). The process in which a relatively monocultural organization is transformed into an organization with room for diversity does not apply only in instances of ethnic variation. Women and older people also must be more appropriately valued for their experiences and knowledge (Marshall, 1984; Veldman and Wittink, 1990).

Teachers who are already teaching at institutions that want to attract students and teachers from ethnic minority groups sometimes see these groups as a problem, using phrases like: "They lack perseverance"; "They drop out"; or "Do we have to know everything about twenty different cultures?" It may be more fruitful to ask whether the institution meets the conditions that allow teachers and students, men and women from different backgrounds, to develop and use their full potential. What is needed is an inventory of the existing possibilities and hurdles if diversity is encouraged to flourish, to see whether and to what degree the organizational culture has opened up to personnel, office workers, and students from different backgrounds (Essed and Reinsch, 1991a and b; Essed and Helwig, 1992). One can identify the following basic tasks in this project (Thomas, 1991):

1. Identify the systems and practices of the educational institution that attract or exclude women and ethnic minorities;

2. Evaluate the educational policy and systems, as well as practices in the educational institution, to see whether they offer sufficient room for diversity;

3. Gain insight into the opinions and experiences of personnel, office

workers, and teachers about existing possibilities for advancement within the institution;

4. Gain insight into the opinions and experiences of students regarding the courses (with respect to cultural diversity).

These tasks can be made operational by translating them into questions pertaining to the actual situation. One can think, among others, along the following lines (Sekaran & Kasner, 1992).

Register and evaluate the administration and teaching staff: It is important to be able to demonstrate to what extent group imbalance is expressed, first, in the organizational structure and administration and, second, in the teaching staff. Questions one could ask are: What is the ethnic and gender profile of the teaching and the office staff? What personnel policy has contributed to it? Is there enough support for the existing teachers to assist them in learning how to recognize and acknowledge relevant differences? Are there sufficient possibilities for advancement for the teachers, administration, and staff of the institution so that diversity can be developed at all levels?

Register and evaluate the student body: What is the ethnic and gender profile of the student body? Is the general recruitment policy such that it can result in a culturally varied student population? Are there good contacts between the institution and the various minority group organizations? What kind of information do new students get? Are they informed about the importance of leadership in culturally mixed organizations throughout their schooling? Is it university policy to make it possible for students to develop the expertise to prevent, reveal, and intervene against discrimination in the policies, procedures, and practices of organizations?

Expand the framework: Can students and teachers sufficiently develop and transmit European and global perspectives on specific issues? White Dutch students may have less experience than ethnic minority students in combining one cultural framework with another. The necessary skills can be taught in the course of their study. With the student body becoming more diverse, teachers also need the skills to supervise constructive controversy, with students invited to elaborate on their own perspectives from different positions and experiential backgrounds. I agree with the view, pointed out by Kouzes and Posner

(1993) that appreciating diversity allows constructive controversy to stimulate innovative thinking, which leaves students much more open-minded and knowledgeable about the subject.

Diversifying is more than toleration of ethnic differences. The institution drops the rigid demands of a uniform organizational culture. Diversifying begins when it is recognized that diversity is a valuable element in achieving excellence. Problems arise not from diversity, as some people think, but from a lack of vision on how to use the various talents, experiences, and expertise and on how to acknowledge multiple identities, interests, and perspectives.

Developing an appreciation of diversity is a process of cultural change, which requires planning, time, and good supervision. As a result, the courses offered and the educational policy become internationally rather than nationally oriented and transcultural rather than monocultural. Furthermore, it requires a personnel policy that allows individual employees more space to develop. The staff involved are asked to reorient existing educational traditions. It is critical to break through the ethnocentric and Eurocentric ways of thinking and to intervene against discrimination.

Ethnocentrism and Eurocentrism

Ethnocentrism, a phenomenon that probably occurs in all cultures, means that people judge other cultures according to their own norms and habits. Examples in daily life abound. People from one culture take a shower twice a day, and think disparagingly of people who traditionally take a bath once or twice a week. Parents who put their children to bed by eight o'clock in the evening, which is often the case in the Netherlands, might criticize situations where children stay up until eleven, which is the case in some Mediterranean countries.

Eurocentrism is a view of humanity that places cultures in an evolutionary perspective, with the model of European progress as the norm, whereby civilization is associated with rationality and control of nature (see also Chapter 3, above). In this way of thinking the (male) Western European is inherently rational and the (female) non-European, emotional (Gilman, 1985). Furthermore, southern cultures are judged in relation to their similarity or dissimilarity with European societies on points considered modern and civilized in the European view: their level of technology, their democracy, their legal systems, and their market economy. Eurocentrism is rooted in the historical dominance of the European model and the ideology connected with it, namely that European civilization may not be perfect but that it is the best in the world so far.

Eurocentric thinking exaggerates the differences between European and other cultures (Robinson, 1983). Because of an overemphasis on regional, linguistic, and cultural differences, there is little room left to explore the many similarities between cultures, or, for that matter, the valuable elements in other cultures. An example of Eurocentrism is the presumption that children normally grow up in monolingual households and learn second languages only in school. In most of the world, however, children grow up with two or more languages and culturally and linguistically mixed environments are considered normal. Eurocentrism is the bedrock of cultural racism.

The Culturalization of Racism

The decolonization after World War II, the horror of the holocaust, and the advance of science have all contributed to changes in the expression of racism in recent years. The idea that there are various human races has long been discredited, and the belief that black people have inferior brains is now only held by white supremacists. Still, racialized thought continues to exist. An example is the word "negro," which is widely used in the Netherlands, a "racialized" label from nineteenth-century racism, which placed Caucasians, Mongoloids, and Negroids in descending order on the biological scale. Even though many people associate racist ideas mainly with this racial hierarchy, racism never referred only to the myth of racial hierarchy.

Ideas about racial differences were also linked with assumed sociocultural characteristics. The colonial "civilization mission" propagated the idea of the superiority of Western culture. As the element of racial hierarchy became latent in European thinking, the idea of cultural hierarchy became more prominent. These days it is considered quite unacceptable to talk about the genetic superiority of the "white race," yet it is quite normal to speak about ethnic minorities from the south as if they were socially or culturally backward—in other words, less civilized. Moreover, dominant representations of ethnic minority cultures are reduced to stereotypes, in which cultures are seen as fixed constellations, as fixed as a genetic structure. Whereas in the nineteenth century,

people from the Third World were considered "backward" in European thinking because of the assumed genetic inferiority, they are now
considered "to be lagging behind" because of the supposed cultural and
social inferiority. From the above, we can conclude that the earlier
biological determinism has found its match in modern-day cultural
determinism.

Getting Rid of Eurocentrism and Racism

The following anecdote is about a well-known experiment and shows
how gender in textbooks can influence children's performance. If you
ask a class with girls and boys to solve a problem in which they have to
calculate how to mix certain elements, you get gender-related results. If
the question is about how much water, sand, cement, and stone it takes
to build a wall, the boys score better than the girls. If the question is
about how much flour, butter, water, and eggs it takes to bake a cake,
the girls score better than the boys. An "ethnic" variation on this experiment is certainly imaginable.

A critical evaluation of textbooks and other materials, as in the example above, is not only important in elementary and high school
education, but also, and especially, in colleges and universities. Questions to ask are: Does the material used provide sufficient insight into
ethnic relationships in society? Do students get sufficient insight into
the historical and social context of Eurocentrism and racism? From
which perspective are courses about ethnic relationships taught? Who
is "we" and who is "they" in them? Is there a major in ethnic studies, or
is such a major being developed? What is the relationship between the
subject of ethnic studies and the practice of ethnic relationships in the
college or university?

In courses in educational management, personnel management, or
labor relations, one can ask questions about the focus in the models of
management and organizational behavior. Which kinds of decision
procedures are advocated? Are there alternatives? What is taught about
conflict management? What role does emotion play in it? Are there
dominant white or male norms, and if so, to what extent are they more
effective than others? To what extent do ethnocentric, Eurocentric, or
male-centered approaches hinder the development of broader-based
knowledge and skills?

Problems may also turn up with respect to the position and status of teachers at the college or university. Relevant questions might be: Are there ethnic divisions in the organizational hierarchy? How does the hiring and selection of teachers take place? Are new colleagues mostly recruited from one circle? Is diversity actually implemented or is it a matter of good intentions, where, in practice, everything stays as it was.

Strategic Planning

It might be helpful to examine the career perspectives of nonteaching staff in institutions of higher learning with regard to the following points:

1. Hiring. Are women and people of color hired on a contract basis, or in permanent jobs (or with the prospect of a permanent job)?

2. Possibilities for promotion. It is important to have a good career policy in place for all employees, regardless of gender and ethnic background. If no such policy is in place, the negative effects may show up in the early stages of the diversifying process. A conflict may arise between a tradition of advancement from within and the decision to obtain diversity, which — certainly in the early phases of the process — often requires the selection of outside candidates. In anticipation of this, the opportunities for women and ethnic minorities within the organization can be enhanced. Promising candidates of color and white women can be "discovered" at an early stage, as often happens with white male candidates. One can, for instance, coach promising students by keeping an eye open for assistantships, conferences that may be of interest, and committee seats in the institution.

3. Decision procedures. Are decisions rigged by being made by a network of like-minded white men? What kind of exclusion mechanisms are at work? How can this pattern be broken?

4. Majority decisions. If this principle goes awry, it can result in "tyranny" by the majority (Guinier, 1994). Teachers and students of color are often outvoted because they are a numerical minority. A first step in getting rid of this pattern is to make people aware of the different concerns and perspectives of the dominant and dominated groups on specific questions.

Ethnic inequality can be reinforced by all kinds of daily interactions. In order to gain insight into this, teachers may reflect on the following points: How do I relate to the students? Which students do I have most/least affinity with and why? Is this a matter of personal preference, or does my affinity coincide with gender and ethnic lines? How do

I evaluate students from different groups? Why do I give some students the benefit of the doubt and not others? Do I intervene against (semi-) racist, sexist, or homophobic jokes or statements in class? Am I equally proud of good results by students of color and white students? Do the examples I use during lectures mostly refer to dominant group experiences or do I use a broader frame of reference?

Students might check the following points: How are (study) groups formed? How do the members of the groups work together? Are the contributions of white male students automatically seen as more valuable than those by male and female students of color? Do students of color have to bow to majority decisions often? Does this interfere with their own development? Is there enough room to bring up personal perspectives? And how is that evident? What is the general reaction to students who bring up racism and want to take courses about it? Does the majority feel accused? Are students who bring up racism criticized and called oversensitive, or are their accounts analyzed and judged according to rational and knowledgeable criteria? (See Chapter 4 above.)

Diversifying: Ten Suggestions

In this last part, I give ten considerations in developing a climate that welcomes diversity in colleges and universities (see also Sekaran & Leong, 1992a). These ideas might also be useful for other organizations to consider.

1. Businesses and institutions in the job market will have to deal with an increasingly diverse work force. They will want to keep the workers of color and the white women they hire, so having good personnel officers, managers, and staff with some experience in working with culturally mixed teams might come in handy. Colleges and universities can prepare students for this situation. They are, after all, the future decision makers who can contribute to improving the quality in management once they are in the workplace. Moreover, managers need to be evaluated on their ability to assume leadership in a climate of diversity.

2. If the managers of the future are going to be required to diversify their scope, there are implications for the colleges and universities. Students may want to take courses in diversity management, thereby granting expert knowledge on labor relations in a multiethnic society the same status as business administration, or economics.

3. Successful diversifying begins with a coherent plan in which the

implementation of the measures within the various levels of the organization is well balanced. It is important for this plan to have the support of top management and essential that middle management is fully responsible for its successful implementation. Therefore it is critically important to develop good communication between the various levels within the institution on this issue.

4. Diversifying is a process in which the institution does not stand alone. Consultation, feedback, and training are recommended. It is sensible to work with human resource advisers in the early phases — just as one might work with financial consultants who can be called upon whenever they are needed.

5. It is important to avoid a situation in which women and representatives from ethnic minorities become token figures in teacher or student groups. Encouraging diversity means more than hiring a single teacher of color. Changes in the organizational culture are important because diversifying can get stuck in stale, inflexible organizational traditions.

6. Students of color and women need recognizable role models just as much as white male students do. It can be a positive development to hire (women) professors and office workers from ethnic minority groups, especially in strategically important positions, so that their work and views are seen to have an influence. After all, it is difficult for students of color to positively identify with a teacher or office worker whose self-esteem is shaky due to the pressure to assimilate they feel from white colleagues. Then again, the history of resistance teaches us that students are in the forefront and may be critical, if not radical, in demanding progressive change, including teachers they can identify with.

7. Diversifying is a gradual process. Good advice at the management level is essential in this process, but so is communication with the teachers, students, and student advisers. Creating sufficient opportunities to evaluate progress at the various institutional levels tends to be effective, especially in the early phases. It is also a good idea to make use of the expertise of the persons involved, for instance, by consulting students and teachers from other cultures.

8. Don't gloss over the problems of racism. Make acquiring knowledge of it a normal part of the educational experience.

9. Everything costs money. Changing mentalities is important in order to make the diversifying process run smoothly, but changing

attitudes is not enough. Investment in changing the personnel structure is required.

10. Developing diversity is not a matter of questions like "Am I racist?" "Am I doing it right?" or "How am I supposed to do this all by myself?" It is about tapping into relevant channels of information as a team. If support is forthcoming from the motivation and knowledge within the organization itself, it is safe to assume that any lack of insight will be temporary. It is always possible to get support from outside specialists who can do anything from screening a course and programs for Eurocentrism to developing methods to broaden support for the process of diversifying.

8

Pioneers among Women of Color

We have come to stay,
and we're going to make it worth our while

"Every now and then I look back to make sure that the traces I leave behind are not misleading others. Since you don't always know who is going to use you as their role model, it is vital to set a good example."

This statement was made by a student leader, a black woman, twenty-one years old, whom I met a few years ago at a university in the United States. Her statement can be interpreted in various ways. It can mean that you always have to be "good" in life. That interpretation focuses on self-interest: Don't let anyone say that I haven't been good. But this student meant something different; as a pioneer she feels responsible for a larger group.

This chapter concerns pioneers among women of color, women who provide political support for each other, who give each other inspiration, power, courage, beauty, and wisdom. Fierceness, resolution, and a strong sense of responsibility are combined with hard work, and the self-confidence you need in order to deal with confrontation.

These pioneers are women who, despite racism and despite discrimination, have gained a place for themselves as women in the job market, in politics, in education, and in the media, and who actively shape the future for women of color. They know that racism exists; that it can't be avoided and that ignoring it won't help. They challenge and overcome the barriers.

Pioneers often risk their own health by working with continuous stress and by giving more of themselves than is good for them. There is hardly any other choice. What women accomplish, is accomplished, despite —

Walking in the footsteps of their ancestors and passing the torch on to new generations, some important questions for pioneering women are:

Where do we stand?
Where are we going?
What are we fighting for?
Where do we get our motivation?
Where do we get the strength?
What are we giving of ourselves for?
In whose footsteps are we following?
What traces are we leaving behind?
And do we feel responsible for this?

I want to place these questions in a transcultural and transnational context — a context that goes beyond the borders of culture or country — where political bonds between women transcend the dividing lines of color, religion, language, and other cultural limitations setting people apart.

Politicizing Experience

For women, everyday life can be a site of political struggle. The kitchen, living room, or doorway of a school becomes a political space where women cooking, drinking coffee, or waiting for the children to get out of school exchange family stories, as well as consult with each other about the future of the children in school. Women act politically whenever they ask questions about a lack of people of color on the boards or teaching staff, whenever they contemplate action against discrimination.

Raising children becomes a political matter whenever a mother, father, grandmother, grandfather, aunt, older brother, or cousin explains to someone younger that, although white people usually have better opportunities in society, this is not always justified. Or when a child is told that people of color do not have to accept a subordinate position and are working to change the situation.

Over the last fifteen years, women of color in the Netherlands have gone through a course in consciousness raising with lightning speed. Only a few, however, had grandmothers, mothers, fathers, or other role models who could teach them about ethnic relationships and discrimination in the Netherlands. Usually, their consciousness was raised as a result of their own experiences. Women recognized themselves in the lives of other people of color and realized that some could be generalized. There were few programs giving information about racism, and textbooks and newspapers were silent on the issue. But women started talking about it themselves and began setting up their own networks and organizations. They became more assertive, developing strategies for gaining more control over their own future.

In addition to organizing within their own groups, one of the most important political developments has been that women have organized themselves beyond ethnic lines (Robles, 1991). True, there are ups and downs; some are more successful than others, but getting together is only a first step. The next question is: What are our plans and goals?

Raised Consciousness

The first sparks of open discontent came from women in the vanguard of the feminist and/or leftist movements. Between 1981 and 1984, in an increasing number of writings and conferences, women of color made it clear that they did not want to become swept away in the waves of the Dutch women's movement. On their agenda the problem of racism was higher than on the white women's agenda.

In 1981, there was a large conference on immigrant women attended by representatives from numerous nationalists. Action was targeted at the areas of work, education, health care, legal position, and the fight against racism. This conference yielded more than a set of demands; it was a place where old contacts were renewed and new contacts were made. In 1983, an enormous push in consciousness raising came from the black women's group in the Winter University. In 1984, the wide publicity around the publication of a book on everyday racism based on the experience and views of black women kept the impetus going (Essed, 1984, 1990b). In the following years, a black women's newspaper appeared, along with a number of existing ethnically oriented magazines. Pioneering women of color organized courses for others who never had the chance to get an education.

In 1985, after thorough preparation, a national center for ethnic minority women, "Flamboyant," opened its doors. This center, subsidized by the city of Amsterdam, was more than just a meeting place. Flamboyant bubbled with life. There were lunchtime discussions and training sessions, a small documentation section and a library for and about women of color. A couple of years later, the city's subsidy was withdrawn and Flamboyant had to close its doors — only to have women build their own organization, Zami, to fill the gap Flamboyant left. In the meantime, there was growing criticism of government policies: women from ethnic groups no longer wanted to be caught in the middle between the minority and women's emancipation policies, but demanded a coherent policy instead, that fit the target group. At a much-discussed national conference about racism and women's history in 1987, women of color presented various anticolonialist papers, also shedding light on the role of women in the history of the liberation struggle in the former colonies and in the 1950s in the Netherlands.

These and other events were mostly concentrated in the big cities, where the majority of the women of color live, but this is changing. For many years, speakers have been traveling all over the country to offer instruction and training. Now assertive women set up their own courses in schools for social work. Slowly but surely, results are becoming visible.

Getting in and Staying There

There is not yet a remarkable trend — only individuals and small groups are involved — but some changes can be seen.

Politics: Yasemin Tümer, the first woman on the national Women's Emancipation Council specifically arguing the case for women of ethnic minority groups, has clearly influenced the Council. The specific consequences of the general women's policies on women of color are now regularly taken into account. A special brochure has been published about the position of ethnic minority women in the job market, including policy recommendations (Emancipatieraad, 1988). Since then, the Council has reserved a seat for an ethnic minority representative.

A few women of color are getting into the city councils as well (Goudt, 1989; Choenni, 1983). They are often in a lonely position, which requires a lot of perseverance and stamina, but these are strong women. Most of them fight for women's issues.

In various cities, women of color are policymakers. These are often short-term or otherwise uncertain jobs, but nonetheless they offer opportunities. In Amsterdam, a woman of color has been the deputy head of the municipal Women's Emancipation Office. Another woman of color became head of the Office of Coordination of Minority Policy.

When she left, she was succeeded by a woman from another ethnic minority group. A few women from former colonies in the Caribbean have become close advisers to the city councils and mayors.

Media: The media, part of the cultural elite, represent key channels through which Dutch norms and values are reinforced and reproduced. They remain fairly impregnable fortresses, but with a great deal of difficulty, some space has been created for presenting a different point of view (Marhé, 1993). Some women have become fixtures in the media: Noraly Beyer, journalist and anchorwoman at NOS; Helen Kamperveen, actress in the soap opera "Medisch Centrum West" [Medical Center West]; Marion Bloem, for, among other things, her documentary films; Gerda Havertong, the actress in the Dutch version of "Sesame Street," is a positive role model for black children and she also gives white children a broader perspective. Behind the scenes a number of women of color are producers. There are also women who have, so far in vain, applied to work for various newspapers and weekly magazines. Some women, however, succeeded by going through alternative channels, such as the Migranten Omroep [immigrant TV].

Job Market: The Netherlands still lags behind in terms of the number of women in the job market. By the end of the 1980s, with a 38 percent participation rate, it surpassed Ireland (36 percent), but Belgium, Italy, Japan, Germany, the United States, and Denmark left it far behind (Bruyn-Hundt, 1988). The Dutch percentage has risen to about 50 percent, but that remains lower than in the surrounding countries. Women are slowly entering lower- and middle-management positions, but top management remains virtually closed to them. So it is quite an achievement for a few women of color to have gotten posts as directors of vocational colleges, as they have, for instance, in Amsterdam. It is remarkable how many people, especially ethnic minority women, are encouraged by this and want to earn their diplomas at these schools. There is a growing number of female doctors and lawyers of color. Small entrepreneurs are starting their own businesses in textile, cosmetics, or hairstyling. There is an increase in the number of women from ethnic minority groups in (freelance) consultant work. The same is true for entertainment, education, nursing, and social services.

There are, however, also troubling developments. Increasingly, women of color get hired to work with clients of color only, while the organization remains white dominated. The question is not just whether women of color participate, but, more important, how. It is more than a matter of numbers; it is also a question of what happens after hiring. Do the organizations change, or do they just add some ethnic "color"? These problems are now recognized and women of color working in white institutions are starting to consult with one another.

Despite the visibility of a number of women in higher positions, 50 percent of ethnic minority women are unable to find a job, despite the tradition of hard work. The figure is 13 percent for white women (Hooghiemstra & Niphuis-Nell, 1995). Studies show that this is not necessarily due only to language problems or lack of education, but also, substantially, because of ethnic discrimination and racism. The government itself does not set a good example here. Statistics show that it hires far too few highly educated people of color. One study of government job ads, all of which stated a preference for ethnic minority candidates, showed that only 12 of the 140 persons hired came from the target group. Direct discrimination as well as indirect discrimination plays a role here. Foreign degrees are often not recognized, and there are not enough courses for people whose proficiency in the language is insufficient. In the meantime, many white Dutch people are starting to believe that color guarantees jobs, unless you're white.

Women workers are also making themselves visible. Fifteen years ago, for example, it would have been unthinkable to publish a brochure on women of color in the cleaning services, because they hardly had access to the required studies and documentation facilities. Now such a brochure has been published by the National Coalition of Organizations of Foreign Workers (LSOBA). It was edited by an ethnic minority woman, who not only pointed out grave difficulties in cleaning services, but also offered information about workers' rights (Voukelatou, 1989).

Education: At the universities, you see young women of color studying to be lawyers, doctors, linguists and literary scholars, educators, psychologists, or political scientists. You can see more and more confident young Turkish, Moluccan, Moroccan, and Chinese women working on their careers. They are pioneers, pathfinders, the advance guard. . . . You hadn't visualized any Surinamese or Antillean women in computer science? Wrong. . . .

More and more women from ethnic groups are going to open universities to brush up on skills or to develop the skills they never had an opportunity to acquire before. For these women, participating in education is a conscious choice, a desire for knowledge. They often have to reorganize their lives in order to come to classes regularly, because many are also responsible for a family and perhaps work in a poorly paid job. Women of color are well represented in training for reentry in the job market. Once that preparation is accomplished, the drive to get a job better than cleaning houses and the decision to return to school turn out to be a big boost to their self-confidence.

I will make a confession at this point: when I started this chapter, I thought to myself, "I'll just summarize the relevant literature on women of color." I came back from my bookcase with a huge pile of publications of which a substantial portion was written by women of color. We have written about women in pioneering positions, about ethnic women's organizations, about meetings and conferences, about education for ethnic minority women, about Surinamese women's organizations, about legal provisions in Turkish and Moroccan divorces. There are autobiographical collections, published interviews with women of various backgrounds, and articles about activist Turkish women. We have written about refugee women, about women of color in social work, about racism, and so on. In short, I found too much for a quick summary. More important is the fact that women of color are getting ahead.

But do women from ethnic groups also play an important role in decision-making procedures regarding the quality of work, education, and the media? Is the system of education, labor relations, politics, and health care changing? The goal is, after all, not to put up tokens of color but to move from the margins to the center of Dutch society. To quote Papatya Nalbantoglu, an immigrant of Turkish background, we can "make a contribution to our shared history and to the freedom of immigrants in a new home country" (Nalbantoglu, 1990, p. 132).

Refueling

Survival, or — more than that — strategic survival, which can take a lot of energy, is both a well of hope and a source of stress. When you get the feeling that you are fighting a losing battle, it is important to recharge in order to remain strong. Strength can be found within ourselves and by identifying with other pioneering women. One must find one's own place at a global and historical level, and develop a transnational orientation to enjoy the inspiration and strength through the courage and power of women elsewhere in the world. This is not only a political matter but also a matter of survival. Those who can reach beyond their own borders are in a stronger position to decide which elements of the Dutch system they want or don't want to internalize. Ethnic minorities are under great pressure to accept without question the dominant norms and values in the Dutch system. I am not suggesting that immigrants should automatically reject norms and values in the Netherlands. Criticizing certain norms and values, regardless of whether they are Dutch, Turkish, Surinamese, Moroccan, or what have you, may bring up the argument "but that is our tradition." That something has been or is a tradition says very little in itself. It is more important to ask whether specific traditions positively contribute to the well-being of people in society, in particular of those who are often denied access to resources. It is better to be aware of traditions and to be open to discussion about them. The power of people to positively contribute to society lies not in keeping traditions for the sake of tradition, but in the capacity to change in the search for a future in which not homogeneity, but cultural diversity will be the norm.

9
Transnationality
The Diaspora of Women of Color in Europe

Multiracism in Europe

It was an ordinary day in December 1955. After a long day of hard work, Rosa Parks, a black woman from Montgomery, Alabama, was too tired to put up with anything anymore. She took the bus home and found herself a seat, happy to finally rest her weary legs. But she hardly got a rest. A white man demanded her seat. Calm and determined, she refused to give it. By doing this, she broke the law. She braved insults, obscenities, and jail, to which she was taken later. She risked violence — her life — but she was firm. Her action was the beginning of a wave of protest, which grew into the civil rights movement in the 1960s (Robinson, 1987).

The 1970s followed with legislative changes guaranteeing equal rights, regardless of color or origin. But in the 1980s, there was a backlash. After ten years of affirmative action, conservatives figured they had gone far enough: social inequality could no longer be blamed on racism, could it!

In 1991, the world — via CNN — was startled by pictures of anger, revolt, frustration, and revenge. Los Angeles was burning. Rage poured out because of a court case. A jury had found a group of white policemen, who had savagely beaten a black man, innocent despite an amateur video recording made by an eyewitness! The events of 1991 indicate that the problem of racism has definitely not vanished. The indignation everywhere, however, from people regardless of their skin

This chapter is a reworking of the inaugural speech I presented at the Black Women's Studies Summer Institute, Frankfurt, 1991.

color, shows that over the years discussion, opposition, and better anti-discrimination legislation have somewhat sensitized public opinion to the problem of racism.

Europe's response to racism is different. In contrast to the United States, in Europe the racism that people of color face is in some sense "new." It is not the same as the traditional forms of racism in the colonized areas at the height of colonialism (Solomos, Findlay, Jones, & Gilroy, 1982). Now it concerns racial and ethnic relations within Europe itself. Up to now, racial hatred in countries such as France, Belgium, Germany, and Great Britain has taken on more violent forms than in the Netherlands (European Parliament, 1985, 1986, 1990; SIM, 1988). With the creation of the European Union, the situation for minorities is rapidly deteriorating, as is evident by the pogroms and increasing violence against Jews, Sinti and Roma (better known as Gypsies), Vietnamese workers, and African students in the various Eastern European countries, as well as the murders of asylum seekers and minorities in Germany. The European politicians react with ambivalence — to put it mildly. So far, no European country has set out on an openly racist course, but neither has any had the courage to fight racism with words and deeds (Parekh, 1988).

Racism is a many-sided problem. One could say *racisms* because manifestations of racism always vary depending on social and political circumstances and the period. Racism in Europe can be placed in the context of neocolonialism and south-north migration, both within Europe and from the former colonies and other Third World countries to Europe. Racism does not pertain to a clearly defined group, but rather to a diverse mixture: people from African and Asian countries colonized by Europe, workers from Turkey, Morocco, and other northern African countries, political and economic refugees from various countries in the south, Sinti and Roma. Europe has developed new forms of exclusion and repression out of old colonial racism, old and new forms of anti-Semitism, anti-Arabism, and xenophobia. Even though not all European countries had colonies, Europe has a common cultural history of racial delusion, remnants of which can still be observed among white extremists.

Racism in Europe

In each European country, racism is unique in its manifestations, but the racisms in the various countries are part of the same European pattern. Below I supply a number of quick sketches that may give an impression of the situation in the countries of Western Europe (in alphabetical order).

Belgium

Despotism, savagery, horrific cruelties, forced labor, mutilation, and murder characterized the Belgian reign of its former colony of Congo, now Zaire (Breman, 1990a and b). In 1960, Belgium left the colony, leaving a trail of blood behind (Merckx & Fekete, 1991). In 1993, 9 percent of almost 10 million inhabitants of Belgium were of foreign origin. On the basis of race, cultural, and class criteria, sharp distinctions are made between immigrants from within the European Union, the United States, Switzerland, and Austria on the one hand, and Turkish, Moroccan, and Tunisian workers on the other. This is also the case in other Western European countries. People of color are looked down on. Non-Belgian passport holders, many of whom are workers from North Africa and Turkey, are pressured to assimilate and have virtually no rights. They can barely get social security benefits, and they have no right to vote. Furthermore, extreme nationalism and racism are threatening the rule of law (Deslé & Martens, 1992) and more and more Belgians are openly hostile toward other cultures, especially Islamic ones (Merckx & Fekete, 1991). Children born to immigrant workers in Belgium are not granted Belgian citizenship, and young men of color are often harassed by the police. In 1991, just as in Paris, Moroccan youngsters rebelled against racism and their systematic marginalization (Hermans, 1991). They expressed anger at the lack of opportunity to create a decent life. Their future does not look much better than their parents' had been, and that generation was never allowed to move beyond menial labor — if they were able to keep their jobs at all during the economic recession of the 1970s and 1980s.

Denmark

The "Islamic invasion" and the "cultural threat from the Third World" are popular topics of conversation in Denmark. Nevertheless, people of color make up less than 2 percent of the whole population — and the majority of them are refugees. Institutionalized racism is not very different from that found in the rest of Europe. There is less violence against minorities than in other European countries, yet there is the usual police harassment of Africans and negative media coverage. Racism is totally denied in Denmark. According to Quraishy and O'Connor (1991), the Danish climate is so repressive that the courts have declared it a criminal libel to state that Denmark is a racist society. This situation is rationalized by using the pseudoscientific argument that only the explicit expressions of the idea of racial hierarchy can be called racism. In this perception of racism, Denmark is not unique. The same is true for the Netherlands and used to be true for Germany. Not until 1992, when racist terror attacks appeared in the international press every day, did the problem of racism gain official recognition. Until then, objections to aggression and discrimination against black Germans and ethnic minorities in Germany were not acknowledged as racism. In public political debate, it was said "One cannot speak of racism, because that would trivialize the suffering of the Jewish people during German fascism" (Kalpaka & Räthzel, 1991, p. 150).

France

France has immigrants from former North African colonies and from the overseas French departments, such as Guadeloupe and Martinique, and together they make up about 7 percent of the population. The so-called threshold of tolerance is a popular theme (MacMaster, 1991). This pseudoscientific notion argues that a city or neighborhood can absorb no more than 10 percent of a "foreign" influence. In consequence of this theory, France has had a dispersion policy for years (Lloyd & Waters, 1991). Apart from anti-Semitism, the French have a virulent form of animosity toward North Africans (van den Brink, Cuartas, & Tanja, 1988). In French political discourse, the position and presence of people of Muslim background are constantly debated (De Wenden, 1991). Immigrants from the former colonies who have French passports enjoy more rights, but they too are confronted with racism. Anti-immigrant violence erupted in Marseille against the Algerians in the early 1970s. In 1991, less than twenty years later, North African youths in Lyon and Paris rebelled against being constantly intimidated and harassed by police. They followed the example of the black British youths in Brixton in 1981.

Great Britain

The German explosion of violence against ethnic minorities in the early 1990s sometimes makes people forget that Great Britain has been the scene of segregation, violence, attacks on and murder of black people for decades (Smith, 1989; Tompson, 1988). In the 1970s, black Britons rose up against discrimination on the job market, poor housing, aggression by the police, and attacks from the extreme right. The government responded with antidiscrimination and equal opportunity legislation. As is often the case after a period of improvement, there was a backlash, which in the 1980s, was expressed among other things in attacks on "antiracism." British racism and reactions to it have been studied extensively. For further discussion, I refer to, among others, Bell and Solomos, 1990; Solomos 1989; Donald and Rattansi, 1992; Braham, Rattansi, and Skellington, 1992.

Italy

Migration to Italy by people from the Third World began later than immigration to most other European countries. The first phase of immigration, from 1970 to 1985, brought people from the former colonies in Africa, Iranian refugees, and workers from the Philippines, Morocco, and Tunisia. More recent groups include Ghanians and people from Senegal, India, Pakistan, and Sri Lanka. Most immigrants and refugees are men, with the exception of domestics from the Philippines and Cape Verde. Italy has close to 1 million emigrants from Africa and is currently accused by other European Union countries of having borders that "leak like a sieve." Italian employers, however, profit hugely from cheap labor, especially when illegal immigrants are concerned. Many Africans, often well-educated people, will work for practically nothing in Italy. They tend to work in agriculture and street trade and accept any wage. Efforts by the Italian government to legalize illegal labor have been unsuccessful. Such attempts meet with opposition by the employers, who expect that legislation in that area will lead to a rise in wages. A growing number of African women become prostitutes. Racial violence, including murder, against Africans occurs regularly. Soon after the first publicized murders of Africans, concerned scholars and journalists started a debate about racism (Balbo & Manconi, 1990, 1992). Italy has taken some progressive initiatives toward developing efficient legislation against discrimination and racism; for example, one government proposal at the end of 1992 included strong measures against public expression of racism.

One could discuss other European countries as well, but I hope that this selected information on racism is enough to make my point: Europe has a problem with racism. Against this background, the rest of this essay focuses on women of color in Europe.

Women in Transnational Contexts

The experiences of women of color transcend national borders in Europe. The first transnational experience is that of being made the Other. Nobody is born as the Other. People are made into the Other. Everywhere in Europe, women of color are labeled as non-European, or as not-really-European. "Where do you come from?" and "When are you going back?" What is back? Some women are first-generation immigrants and have memories of a country of origin. But many were born in Europe and the only home they have is a European country.

A second transnational experience has to do with the belittling and denial of everyday racism in all of the European countries. Racism, as one author stated, is Europe's public secret (Bhavnani, 1992). Under moral pressure from the international community and the threat of divestment by, among others, the United States, Germany has become the first country to admit its racism. Politicians from various other countries continue to point at each other in a game where nobody dares to be the first one to intervene against the downward spiral of racism. From England to France and from Italy to the Netherlands, a country's politicians claim to represent the most tolerant nation in Europe (van Dijk, 1993). The Netherlands have made tolerance a national trademark and lectures Germany. German politicians spoke, until 1991, about "Ausländerfeindlichkeit," this is xenophobia. But about racism? No, things weren't quite as chaotic as over there in England! British politicians see their country as the most tolerant and civilized nation in Europe — or rather the world. They condemn the vulgar racism in Italy. Italian politicians, in turn, feel that tolerance toward immigrants is a fact because they will never forget that their own people were once looked down upon when they migrated to work in northern Europe. They are annoyed by French excesses. . . .

A third transnational experience is the process of political awareness. Many women of color take inspiration from the writings and political actions of black people in the United States, in particular the contributions of women. When the systematic nature of ethnic marginalization is trivialized, it helps to be able to recognize a similar situation in the struggle of women beyond your own borders. The initial lack of insight into European racism has had a number of positive consequences: women of color in Europe had to look beyond their own ethnic groups at an early stage, and they found a voice in women from the United States such as Angela Davis, Audre Lorde, Michelle Cliff, bell hooks, Chandra Mohanty, Trinh T. Minh-ha, Patricia Hill Collins, Gayatri Chakravorty Spivak, and others. Thus, they created transnational role models and transnational heroines. After all, why should one group, or country, have the exclusive right to be proud of the heroes it has produced? When you were able to interpret your own situation using insights gained by women on the other side of the Atlantic who have had similar experiences, it is also easier to recognize and compare experiences of women of color who are close neighbors in Europe. British women of African, Asian, and Caribbean origin have formed coalitions (Bryan, Dadzie, & Scafe, 1985). So have women of Caribbean, Turkish, Moroccan, Moluccan, and Indonesian origin in the Netherlands (Zamikrant, 1992). These coalitions are not perfect — with them there are struggles over identity. Nevertheless, women are capable of staying in contact, negotiating, and reaching out beyond ethnic and racial borders. This is true for coalitions with women of color, and also for progressive cooperation with white women (Babel & Hitipeuw, 1992; Cense, 1991).

It would be wrong to assume that women of color have to feel or act as one, because there are differences in their cultural background and experiences, differences in class and education, differences in age and sexual orientation. Therefore it is neither useful to unite on the basis of identity, nor to unite only on the basis of the shared experience of being a victim of racism. Women of color do not necessarily have the same identities, but it is useful to unite and cooperate, regardless of color or ethnic origin, to achieve specific goals, that is, to bring about equal rights and justice for all women and for all people from ethnic minority groups.

Gender and Racism

There is little research on European representations of women of color. Such European representations would probably include notions of cultural "disadvantage," because it is often assumed that people from the Third World encounter a world much superior to their own when they come to Western Europe (Memmi, 1965; Roemer, 1995). Furthermore there is evidence that women of color are perceived as exotic, sexually available, or aggressive (Essed, 1984, 1991; Da Lima, 1988; Pheterson, 1986). Generally, however, paternalistic attitudes prevail, wherein it is believed that the emancipation of Third World women, women of color, and female immigrants is lagging behind the emancipation of white women (Essed, 1982, 1989; Loewenthal, 1984). In addition, it is not unlikely that images of women of color, and specifically women of African origin, are strongly influenced by United States culture, through literature, television series, and many movies.

An important difference between the experiences of women of European origin and those of immigrants from the south concerns the family. Feminist theory has criticized those aspects of the social order and the institution of the family that maintain gender inequality (among others, Oakley, 1974; Barrett, 1980). This view is shared by northern critics as well as by those from Asian, African, and Caribbean countries (among others, Lindsay, 1980; Jayawardena, 1982; Mies & Reddock, 1982; Nash & Safa, 1989). The family, however, whether nuclear or extended, cannot be seen only in terms of its repressive nature. For immigrants whose cultures are not respected and valued in the rest of society, the family also provides a place where they can enjoy the familiar and traditional. Family ties, both with relatives in the country of residence and with relatives in the country of origin, often are one of the few sources of emotional, social, and economic support immigrants have. But immigration laws form a threat for their family life. The constitution protects and preserves the integrity of the family, usually considered the pillar of society. When European laws and regulations are applied to immigrants from the south, however, they have a destructive effect on existing or potential family ties. Time and time again, the governments attempt to come up with new restrictions to prevent children, parents, partners, or lovers from joining their fathers, mothers, daughters, sons, husbands, wives, or fiancées in Europe.

Take, for instance, the following example of a black woman, a mother.

During an international conference in France, "Women and Racism," a group of women of various ethnicities and nationalities has met for dinner. We are discussing that day's sessions, and the situation in our various countries. One white woman from Switzerland talks about the difficulties involved in setting up a kindergarten for refugee children. Even after the class began, the police continued to harass them. "Sometimes you don't know if a child will come back the next day." As she is telling this story, a British woman of Afro-Caribbean background who is also there is silently weeping and tears run down her cheeks; she is in her early thirties. We are worried and ask her what is wrong. We have come to know her as an active participant who raised major points with much commitment. As she wipes away her tears with the back of her hand, she laughs a little by way of apology. "It's all right. I didn't mean to cry. Don't mind me. Everything is okay. . . ." When we insist that she explain, she says that she is not sure whether her lover and partner, the father of her seven-month-old baby, will still be there when she gets back to England from France. He does not have a residence permit. Like millions of other immigrants and refugees this family lives with the daily fear of police raids and deportation.

This is Fortress Europe. It doesn't matter whether you were born here or not, whether you have children or not. We all know something of the experience this woman is talking about and it will be repeated in the future.

Another question that affects women of color is population policy. The poverty, hunger, and environmental problems in the world are often attributed to the overpopulation of the Third World. Even though they take place in very different geographical places, the forced sterilizations of women in Bolivia or in India and of women of color in the United States and Europe are all manifestations of the view that people of color and the poor in the south are a threat to the survival of (white people in) the north (Chase, 1980). In a number of European countries, abortion rights have been rescinded out of fear of white depopulation. At the same time, neither effort, nor money, nor energy, nor the environment are spared in order to develop refined artificial reproductive technologies, possibly at the expense of the health of (white) women (Baruch, D'Adamo, & Seager, 1988; Overall, 1989). The underlying racism in these tendencies becomes clear when one considers the illogic of increasingly rigid immigration laws, at a time when Europe is heading straight toward a labor shortage. The global discourse and practice of population politics illustrate exceptionally well that nationalistic, racist, and sexist ideologies evoke and reinforce each other (Seidel, 1988; Yuval-Davis & Anthias, 1989; Saghal & Yuval-Davis, 1992).

Overcoming European Borders

Europe, today and tomorrow, is and will be a Europe of different minorities: racial, cultural, national, regional, religious, and linguistic. Moreover, today's refugees are tomorrow's potential minorities, which means that one cannot divorce race and ethnicity in Europe from the north-south context at the global level.

We have entered a phase in history where the nation-state will no longer be the most relevant socioeconomic unit (Mohanty, 1991). The world order is increasingly controlled by multinational companies, multinational financial institutions, and multinational political bodies (Race & Class, 1992). Furthermore south-north and east-west migrations have created a reality more complex than the image of the "rich and evil" north and the "poor and innocent" south. The number of impoverished and homeless people is growing in the north. There are also unbelievably rich elites in the south, who profit because they pay almost nothing for labor and are able to live like gods and goddesses in Brazil, India, and other places. The relationship of the south to the north is no longer just geographical, because the south now also exists within the borders of the north. Fortress Europe, the aggressiveness of the European political climate, and increasing violence against minorities all point to the fact that the iron curtain that once cut through Europe is now placed around Europe. People of color and other ethnic minorities will have to fight assertively for their rights to prevent Fortress Europe from becoming Prison Europe. In this struggle, it is important for dissidents and opponents to look beyond the borders of Europe. People of color in the north have a southern heritage, though many were born in the north. But people of color who live in the north are also part of the north, upholding its standard of living which depletes the natural resources, which leads directly or indirectly to the death, oppression, and marginalization of millions of people in the south.

To illustrate this point, take the following situation: at the airport in Manilla, the Philippines, a woman is standing in line to check in. She is in her twenties. Since we are both early, we talk to each other as we lean against the check-in counter. At first she had addressed me in Tagalog, because she thought I was from the Philippines myself. When we switch to English, she explains that this is her first flight. She is going to work as a maid for a rich family in Israel, she says. Slightly alarmed, I ask if she knows anybody there. Yes, her cousin is already there. She is silent for a while and then she admits that she is afraid to travel, especially because she has to change planes twice. I advise her to look for the "transfer" signs. She will manage, I am sure. She is going to earn money so that her family can survive and her children will have more opportunities than she did.

She is on her way to Israel, but she could well be on her way to a rich family in Italy. She could have been lured into prostitution by a German. She thinks that she won't see her partner and three small children for three to five years — if she ever sees them again. When it is her turn, she is told she was standing in the wrong line. Ironically, her future employers have sent her a first-class ticket. They are obviously not cheap. Like a traditional bride, she may feel like the queen of the ball for the duration of the flight, but the pain of separation from her country and family will not be erased by the first-class champagne and caviar.

This is a personal drama in a transnational context. It is the story of many women from the south, who, driven by poverty, are forced to leave behind their mothers, grandmothers, children, fathers, and partners in order to help the family survive.

Women who are fleeing economic misery, sexual violence, or political oppression find the Third World they had hoped to leave behind when they reach Europe. Take, for example, the many women who work in ethnic sweatshops in the garment industry. Due to economic recession and discrimination on the job market, increasing numbers of Asian, Turkish, and other immigrants have started their own businesses. Often men hire women to work for them without pay or for very low wages. This arrangement fits into the patriarchal structure of various ethnic communities, but there is more to it. The men as well as the women are confronted with restrictions in the job market as a result of discrimination and economic stagnation (Phizacklea, 1990). In addition, married women are in a vulnerable position due to the sexist immigration laws in some European countries, where they lose their residency permits if they divorce their husbands.

There are also women who migrate on their own in order to create better opportunities. The fact that women do not just migrate as the dependents of their husbands is shown by the increasing number from the south and from Eastern Europe who end up, more or less voluntarily, in prostitution or as the victims of trafficking (Launer, 1991; Pheterson, 1986). Take, for instance, the following story, which takes place in Brazil. It is about a girl who is no more than thirteen years old, who is one of many poor whites from the northeastern part of Brazil. She sells sodas on the beach. Each morning, she drags a heavy cart loaded with drinks across the sand and stays there until about 6:00 P.M. While she is selling drinks, she looks after a few undernourished brothers and sisters. She is scarcely aware of the fact that her figure is developing curves which are visible through the worn bikini she wears every day. At about 4:00 P.M., she takes a break. She dives in the water and has fun playing with some boys of her own age. Aside from shy smiles, she hardly communicates with anyone except the other kids who are selling drinks.

One day, she is so excited that she starts talking. She enthusiastically tells me that she is going to Switzerland. A rich German man is taking her with him. He wants to send her to school. "Does your mother know about this?" I ask. Her parents are poor farmers who live some distance from the city. "Yes," she says. The German man invited them to the city to talk to them. He is paying for a few days in a hotel for them. "They are in that hotel," she says, pointing somewhere far away. But does she know this German man? Yes, he was here last year too. Enthusiastically, she repeats several times that she will be in an airplane, soon. Then she runs away again.

I cannot forget her story. I try to imagine a German man taking a tomboy, probably still a virgin and hardly educated, to Switzerland with him to send her to school. To school?! I decide to take along a pen and paper the next day and ask for her address in Switzerland. I can always write and see how she is doing. Naive of me. The next day, she doesn't show up. Obviously, the German man has quickly finished his business.

What happened to this girl? Did she land in the forced prostitution one hears about so often — an illegal alien, afraid of the immigration service? Is she in a place where she will never be able to recoup the money the "gentleman" paid for her flight to Europe?

Europe is shutting its political gates to the south. At the same time, the economy is strongly dependent on underpaid immigrant labor. The population growth in most European countries is slowing down. Even the presence of the pope has not prevented Italy from having the lowest birth rate in Europe (Kazim, 1991). Who is going to pay for the pensions of all the people in Europe, whose life expectancy is longer than ever? Will new clothes be affordable without the often illegal sweatshops in Amsterdam and elsewhere in Europe? Can we still afford to eat out if restaurant kitchens can no longer take advantage of the work of underpaid and/or illegal cooks and dishwashers? How will the rich Italian women do without their underpaid — sometimes even university-educated — maids from the Philippines or Cape Verde? What will happen to the European standard of living if we really embrace the position that the environment in the south should no longer be destroyed? Will we still have cheap coffee or tea if we make an issue of the protectionism by the rich counties, which artificially keeps prices low and unprofitable for the south? With these arbitrary and simple examples, I want to emphasize that we are citizens of the world and that it is important to place our own situation in a larger context.

Women of Color: Fighters, Pioneers, Successes

Women of color and immigrant women have their own herstories of empowerment and resistance. Hundreds of women from the Caribbean fought in World War II (Bousquet & Douglas, 1991). They voluntarily joined the Auxiliary Territorial Service, the female section of the Territorial army. In the 1970s and 1980s women of color joined white women in the peace movement (Brown, 1983). They protest the racism implied in the overrepresentation of men of color in the casualties of the wars Europe and the United States fight against countries in the south (Terry, 1984). The war against Iraq was an example of this. Women in Europe can learn from the courageous mothers in Argentina, who, despite repression, continued and still do continue to demand to know what has happened to their families. Their actions have inspired and encouraged many women elsewhere.

Women of color have also accomplished much in Europe, despite patriarchal relations in their own communities, and despite racism.

As early as the 1920s and 1930s, women from the Caribbean went to Europe to get degrees in medicine, law, and other professions at a time when it was unusual for women to study (Stam, 1988). There is no doubt that in doing so, they contributed to their own emancipation and to that of women of European origin.

In feminist theory inside and outside Europe, the contributions of women of color have had a significant impact on concepts and theoretical frameworks that were once the domain of white middle-class women (Collins, 1990; Mohanty, 1991; McLaughlin, 1990). Authors from the United States have shown how black women served as a bridge between black rights and women's rights (Giddings, 1985). Criticism and discussion have led to broadening such topics as "the oppression of women," "the family as a place of oppression," and "socialization" (Carby, 1982, 1987). Women of color have questioned the political meaning of the term "we" in feminist theory and, in the Netherlands, identified racism as the cause of a rift in the women's movement (Essed, 1982; Loewenthal, 1984, 1988; Pattynama, 1987). Women have also made contributions to theories about the complex relations among various systems of domination, especially patriarchal relations, imperialism, and racism (Amos & Parmar, 1981; Parmar, 1982; Carby, 1982). Studies have been published on racism targeted at women and the efforts made to overcome it (Bryan, Dadzie, & Scafe, 1985). New theoretical and methodological dimensions have been introduced. Patricia Hill Collins conceptualized historical and contemporary expressions of black feminist thought (1990). I share her tribute to knowledge emerging from concrete experiences in my analysis of *Everyday Racism* (1984, 1991). Alice Walker's visionary concept of womanism urges us to transcend women's issues and to aim at protecting humanity as a whole — women, men, and children.

Women of color in Europe are pioneers in a process that will turn into a civil rights movement. In the 1980s, the actions and publications by black women got the discussion about Afro-German people started (Opitz, Oguntoye, & Schultz, 1986/1991). Women of color in the Netherlands also began organizing and talking about the problem of getting racism onto feminist and nonfeminist agendas (Essed, 1984, 1990a and b; Kempadoo & Loewenthal, 1986). In the United Kingdom, black women were in the forefront of actions against discrimination in the schools (Bryan et al., 1985). They were the ones who defended the rights of children and protected them against teachers who treated them indifferently or negatively.

Their many actions and publications gave women of color the expertise they needed for entry into political institutions. A number represent political parties in Great Britain, Italy, and the Netherlands, and even at the European level (Goudt, 1989). In various European countries, women of color are fighting violence against women within and beyond their communities (Deug, 1990). Lesbians of color have challenged homophobia in society and in their own ethnic groups.

Women are attempting to deal with cultural and national differences in a constructive manner, by keeping common goals in mind. There are positive models of cooperation: transnational, across the borders of countries, and transcultural, across lines of cultural and ethnic groups, and across heterosexual and lesbian divisions. One does not have to be in complete agreement in order to work together politically. And differences in age, class, sexual preference, language, religion, and nationality do not necessarily have to conflict (Young, 1990). The importance of the social, cultural, or personal experiences individuals identify with can change as new insights and experiences replace earlier ones. The process of identification is flexible, because each of us has several sources and experiences we relate to. We all have overlapping experiences and multiple identities.

It is important to combine bonds formed on the basis of common racial and cultural experiences with transnational and transcultural politics and strategies of cooperation. This means making room for the power that emerges from sharing cultures and experiences and for the power that emerges from drawing from one's own specific cultural or personal characteristics within such cooperation. The new Europe will be a Europe of cultural variation, and women will be the pioneers in the transition; our mode of living will not be one of tolerating difference, but one of accepting diversity.

The twenty-first century is likely to be the century of ethnic struggle. On one hand, politicians from various countries have all claimed to represent the most tolerant nation of Europe. On the other hand, people of color in various countries believe the situation they live in is more repressive than in any other country, and thus deserves most attention. It doesn't make much sense to compare bad with bad and worse with worse. We can learn from each other's experiences with strategies, policies, and movements in the various countries.

In Europe, especially in countries where English is the first or second language, women of color have more often compared themselves to black people in the United States than to the worldwide diaspora of women of color. We need more balance in this. Western European and United States ethnic relations are often direct reflections of global north-south relations. A worsening of north-south relations will have more direct consequences for people of color in Europe and the United States than ever before. We cannot overlook that the standard of living and the luxury that we demand in Europe will have adverse consequences for the south. By addressing this problem, political action will become action in a transcultural and transnational framework, beyond the borders of Europe.

10

Teaching in an Age of Diversity

Recently I had an interesting discussion with a Canadian colleague, a professor in the social sciences, about our experiences in academe. We both live in societies where it is extremely rare to have women of color teaching at the university level (Bannerji, Carty, Dehli, Heald, & McKenna, 1991). It turned out that she was using some of my work on everyday racism in the Netherlands and the United States in her courses, and she told me that her students were quite amazed about the similarities between Dutch racism and what was happening in Canada.

Not surprisingly, we also discovered that we had many insights and experiences in common, as immigrants, as academics, and as feminists. Her parents came from Trinidad, mine came from Suriname. We both migrated to the north as teenagers. We exchanged, compared, and discussed these similarities and other parts of our identities and life stories.

Although it was the first time we met, our mutual understanding and immediate sense of sisterhood transcended our differences in nationality and ethnicity. This encounter reminded me how much my own intellectual and political development has been influenced by women of color elsewhere. I read their work, pondered their experiences, and often identified and used their publications in my courses.

I welcome the opportunity to look back, in the course of this chapter, on ten years of teaching on the crossroads of women's studies and ethnic studies. I use the concept of "Women's Studies" simply to refer to all areas of academic concern pertaining to women's and gender issues and "Ethnic Studies" to refer to the whole interdisciplinary field concerned

An earlier version of this chapter was published as "Making and Breaking Ethnic Boundaries: Women's Studies, Diversity, and Racism," *Women's Studies Quarterly*, nos. 3 & 4 (1994): 232–249. Copyright © 1994 by The Feminist Press at The City University of New York.

with race and ethnic relations. The aim is to find common grounds on which women can identify and build new cultural spaces across the ranges of social boundaries which "otherwise" divide us. In doing so I also comment critically upon these otherwise dividing boundaries to show that many of the social realities one takes for granted may turn out to be less certain after being analyzed within a framework of dominance.

Realizing that one cannot be exhaustive on the politics of women's studies/ethnic studies in one essay, I have selected three critical areas of concern.

First, I address the *reproduction of racial and ethnic boundaries* and focus on racism in Europe. It is important to discuss this issue, because racism is embedded in the political context of teaching programs and it is manifested within our universities as well. I take note of the cultural-ization of racism and of everyday racism in the academy.

Second, I attend to the *need to make implicit boundaries explicit* in order to challenge them: racial boundaries, disciplinary boundaries, national boundaries, and ethnic boundaries. I discuss the underlying racial dimensions of the academy and the problems involved in teach-ing about emotionally charged issues such as race and racism.

Third, my argument moves on to look at efforts to *break through boundaries*. This section starts with a brief discussion of women's writ-ings on racism and includes critical views on feminist theory. Subse-quently, I examine academic (feminist and nonfeminist) responses to the quest for ethnic recognition. In doing so I focus particularly on pitfalls of multiculturalism.

Finally, venturing beyond feminism in the north, I suggest that wom-en's studies in Europe encourages students to foster a global perspective on race, ethnic, and gender issues. I develop the implication of con-structive dialogue on the basis of feminist theory in the north and feminist theory developed in the South.

I will use experiences I have had while researching and teaching in the Netherlands to illustrate this chapter. Some of the points I am going to make, however, will also have a wider application.

The Reproduction of Racial and Ethnic Boundaries

Racism in Europe

It is regrettable that at the end of the twentieth century, racism and ethnicism are emerging as the primary areas of conflict in Europe and are guaranteeing the agenda for the century to come. People of color in Europe experience increasingly overt and virulent racism (European Parliament, 1985, 1986, 1990; SIM, 1988; IRR, 1991). The calls for a white Europe are getting louder and with them the view that a white Europe be reproduced through the wombs of white women. The connection between controlling population through immigration policies, on the one hand and through reproductive policies, on the other, can be inferred from the fact that in various European countries restrictions on abortion rights during the past ten years have been closely tied to European entry restrictions. Notably, in Germany legal restrictions in both areas were pushed through almost simultaneously: in May 1993, new rigid immigration laws were followed within two days by a parliamentary decision declaring abortion illegal.

With the 1992 Treaty of Maastricht and the earlier Schengen Agreement (1985 and 1990), Fortress Europe has become a reality, most notably in its hostility to "foreigners," making it a fertile ground for random as well as organized racist attacks. In this sense, European nationalism may well be seen as a racialized nationalism (Bhavnani, 1992). The Schengen countries (Germany, France, Belgium, the Netherlands, and Luxemburg) signed an agreement to "harmonize" policy on visas and to coordinate crime prevention and search operations, in particular with respect to narcotics, explosives, and the registration of hotel guests. A common list is being drawn up of aliens classified as "undesirables," refugees and asylum seekers who are refused entry or residence, and criminals wanted for prosecution. People on this list will be refused entry to all Schengen states (Bunyan, 1991). This equation of crime with refugees and asylum seekers, many of whom are from countries in the south, is common to all European Union countries, whether or not they signed the Schengen Agreement. With the Schengen Agreement in effect, institutionalized racism is likely to be reinforced. Its legal application can lead to discriminatory police actions, which can have a detrimental effect on human rights, in particular those of people who are taken for non-European on the basis of skin color and other physical characteristics.

Immigration policies and processes are not gender neutral. Many women refugees have been sexually abused during wars, in detention, and/or by state bureaucrats. Yet, the violation of a woman's sexual integrity is not considered grounds for refugee status in Fortress Europe (with the recent exception of women from former Yugoslavia). In much political as well as everyday discourse, being "black" or "Third World" and being or becoming European are viewed as "mutually exclusive" (Bhavnani, 1992, p. 15). The belief that people of color have no right to be in Europe is demonstrated by more than the strengthening of the European borders. People of color are confronted on a daily basis with the effects of Eurocentric and racist parliamentary and media debates filtered "down" into the streets, neighborhoods, schools, and work. Take for instance the following scene:

> Riding my bike on a sunny Sunday afternoon in Amsterdam I come to a traffic light and see a woman in the middle of the crosswalk while the traffic light is red. Probably in her mid-forties, she is white, dressed in a fashionable skirt with a matching loosely fitting blouse. She is gesticulating with her arms and saying things I cannot yet hear. At first I think that she must be mentally disturbed, because I know there is an alternative shelter project for people "mad enough to escape from the madhouse," as the sign on top of the building reads, in that particular neighborhood. Nearing the crosswalk I get a clearer view of what is happening. The woman is yelling things at two young white women police officers in a car, who are waiting for the lights to turn green. Next to the police car, at a tram stop, there is a man of color, probably about forty, also fashionably dressed. He is blankly staring at the agitated woman, who is pointing at him. This is what I hear the woman saying to the police officers:
>
> "Well let him produce his passport. Ask him. Let him show it. He is a foreigner, isn't he! So, you are supposed to ask for his papers. What are you waiting for. Ask him. Who the hell does he think he is, saying things to me?" And louder: "*I insist that you ask for his passport.*"
>
> Having come to a stop now myself, close to the woman, I notice that she appears quite sane. She has judged this man on the basis of his skin color and perhaps his accent—but I do not know that—and has concluded that he is an alien and, "therefore," probably illegal as well. Moreover, she is urging that the police catch and, since she believes him to be illegal, by implication, deport him too. Nothing the man may have said to her justifies her resorting to racism in revenge. Even more amazing is the fact that she boldly "orders" the police officers to enforce what she feels is the law, as if she were representing the Dutch State in person.

Obviously, the woman must be held individually responsible for her actions. However, her statements cannot be disconnected from the larger context in which they were made, which has to do with the ongoing parliamentary debates on immigrants and illegal labor. Because of the Dutch experience during the Second World War, when the Germans used Dutch identity registration files to facilitate the deportation of Jews, the Dutch have resisted any parliamentary attempts to introduce compulsory identity cards in the Netherlands for decades. Recently, however, the parliament successfully passed a law requiring that citizens identify themselves at work upon demand of the authorities. The law was introduced as one of a number of procedures against illegal workers.

One can hardly avoid interpreting the woman's request that the man show his ID as coinciding, in an everyday situation, with the Dutch and European parliamentary discourse in which color is connected to crime and corruption. What has been called elite racist discourse (van Dijk, 1993) is absorbed into people's common sense (Lawrence, 1982) and played out in the streets, in the neighborhoods, and at work and elsewhere. This is hardly surprising, given the frequency with which national and European state officials, the media, and bureaucrats suggest that people of color, refugees and asylum seekers alike, are a problem. Scenes such as the one I related are not incidental. Racism is embedded in the political, social, and economic context of all European countries. These realities affect the teaching context in colleges and universities, because students and teachers alike are part of both the university and the wider world. They participate in public life, read newspapers, and form their own opinions about their academic experiences. This pointed out, it is relevant to pay attention to its manifestations in university settings.

Everyday Racism in Academe

There is no fundamental difference between racism in the street and racism in professional settings. In both environments the same mechanisms operate to marginalize and stigmatize ethnic groups and to repress opposition against racism (Essed, 1991; Bannerji et al., 1991). The (predominantly) middle-class values the university represents, such as the common sense appeal to reason, may usually take "the rough edges off, but the impact is no less severe" (Carty, 1991). Open racism such as racial jokes, slurs, and other racist talk are, however, not uncommon as can be inferred also from my own research (Essed, 1991, 1993).

For my book *Understanding Everyday Racism,* I interviewed highly educated black women from the United States and the Netherlands. Traditionally, black women have considered education a key element, if not the most important one for advancement in society (Sokoloff,

1992). Yet, there are a number of structural problems women of color face in higher education and in obtaining and keeping jobs. First, the lack of "role models" puts them at a disadvantage compared to white women (Carroll, 1982). Women of color are underrepresented in relevant positions, such as at the higher levels of the university administration, on the editorial boards of mainstream journals, and on committees awarding scholarships or research grants. Second, they are routinely underestimated and do not get the same promotional advances as white women (Sokoloff). Women of color are confronted with glass ceilings in a more rigid way than white women are. They have to meet higher demands than any other group. They have to be better qualified, more articulate, and more aggressive; they need more stamina to face inevitable set-backs and fewer opportunities for promotion (Fullbright, 1986).

Racism, Victimization, and Responsibility

Below the surface of academic cordiality there may be strong emotions about racial and ethnic issues, but neither guilt feelings from white women nor cynicism from women of color (no white can be trusted) are constructive in the learning process. Moreover, it must not be assumed that all whites are agents of racism and that all people of color are victims. Such a rigid view of the problem ignores the psychology of being oppressed (Fanon, 1967; Meulenbelt, 1985), as well as the fact that even members of dominated groups can engage in racist behavior. Conversely, it is also relevant that many members of the dominant group incidentally or frequently oppose racism, whether in small or in significant ways (Mullard, 1984; Terry, 1975).

In the courses I teach on racism, I emphasize individual responsibility in relation to the outcome of group processes instead of factors such as "fault," "guilt," or "powerlessness." The notion of responsibility for one's actions (Lukes, 1974, 1986) is relevant to make the distinction clear between the structural beneficiaries of racism and the actual agents of racism in everyday situations. Depending on what is at stake, and costructured along class and gender lines, members of the dominant group benefit from racism, whether or not they are aware of this and/or willingly accept this. Let me give a fictitious example. A white woman known to be committed to the struggle against racism applies for a position as a Dutch representative in an international committee.

The application committee favors her above another Dutch candidate, a woman of color, who is in fact more qualified on several grounds. The white woman is only sufficiently qualified, but looks more representative of Holland in the eyes of the committee. The white woman may never even come to know that she was appointed due to positive discrimination to her advantage and negative discrimination against a woman of color and she cannot be held personally responsible for the decision. Nevertheless, it is relevant that we make explicit the implicit racial boundaries so that those who benefit from them will be compelled to acknowledge their advantage.

Making Implicit Boundaries Explicit

Feminist Criticism and the Struggle against Racism

Many of us are familiar, at least through literature and the mass media, with the women's movement in the United States.

> Twice in the history of the United States the struggle for racial equality has been midwife to a feminist movement. In the abolition movement of the 1830s and 1840s and again in the civil-rights revolt of the 1960s, women experiencing the contradictory expectations and stresses of changing roles began to move from individual discontents to a social movement in their own behalf. Working for racial justice, they developed both political skills and a belief in human rights which could justify their own claim to equality. (Evans, 1980, p. 13)

In some of the European countries, progress was made in the opposite order — from feminism to antiracism. In the Netherlands and in Germany a number of women of color who were involved in the feminist and/or lesbian movement during the 1970s and 1980s, started to organize separately as "Blacks." Black feminist criticism and the subsequent emergence of research occurred in three major areas: (a) the critical analysis of key concepts in feminist theory; (b) the study of experiences of (gendered) racism; and (c) the historical continuity of black women's resistance (Knowles & Mercer, 1992). Through their political actions, women of color have made themselves visible.

Writings and political actions by women of color have shifted the frameworks of what were once white middle-class concepts in feminist theory, such as "patriarchy," "the family," and "reproduction"

(Carby, 1982; Parmar, 1982). Their writings generated some critical self-reflection on the part of white feminist scholars (Brittan & Maynard, 1984; Barrett & McIntosh, 1985; Ramanzanoglu, 1989). We are now entering a stage were white women/feminists take up the challenge to explore the racialization of white identity (Brah, 1992). Various recent publications address the way white women experience their gender, class, and sexuality through race (Caraway, 1991; Chaudhuri & Strobel, 1992; Cock, 1992; Ware, 1992; Frankenberg, 1993). White feminists in the academy are using the tools they have acquired to analyze their own "social geography of race" in critical, politicized modes. They are giving priority to antiracism and teaching it in their classrooms, hoping that they can make a difference (Caraway). Teaching is one thing, changing university racial power structures, however, is quite another.

Racialized Realities and Academe

Intersections of race, ethnicity, and gender are often taken to be relevant only with respect to women of color, in the same way as "gender" is often used as an alternative for "women," in such phrases as "gender issues," as if only women have gender. Irrespective of personal preferences and identities, all of us, "black" and "white," men and women, are positioned in racialized and gendered conditions, because race, ethnicity, and gender are fundamental organizing principles of social relations in our society (Omi & Winant, 1986; Anthias & Yuval-Davis, 1992).

A classroom is a racialized situation. Students' experiences are shaped by where they fit in the matrix of race, ethnicity, and gender. The classroom setting is embedded in the wider social system in which racism as ideology is present in everyday activities. Ideology includes all the concepts, ideas, images, and intuitions that provide the framework of interpretation and meaning for racial thought in society, whether systematically organized in academic discourse or in casual, everyday, contradictory, ambivalent, common-sense thinking (Hall, 1986). There is a basis we share: as student and scholar we are both part of the university. But the very common ground we share is racialized and ethnicized because of group differences in the specific histories, affiliations, and spaces the dimensions of race and ethnicity occupy in our lives. The racialized dimensions of the situation may affect the learning process of students differently. All students, however, can make a valuable contribution to exploring further intersections of race, gender, and ethnicity in society, drawing also from their own subjectivity, meaning their own experiences placed in the physical, political, and historical context of their lives (Ellis & Flaherty, 1992).

Contested Boundaries in Scholarship: Teaching about an Emotionally Charged Topic

In teaching in the European context at the crossroads of women's studies and ethnic studies, we face many problems. Among these are the serious underrepresentation of students and scholars of color at colleges and universities and the emotionally charged nature of the subjects. On one hand, there are problems involved with getting financial support for a program that may be considered "too political," and, on the other hand, problems involved when radicalized women of color reject the program as "too moderate." There are problems related to the denial and trivialization of racism in all of the European countries.

Does this mean that we cannot build on any of the achievements of feminist scholars elsewhere? Against the idea that we must start from scratch one can argue that the United States, for instance, has something to offer with respect to a pedagogy of ethnically inclusive feminist theory (Kibbelaar, in press) and that we can learn from the United States experience. To a certain degree we can surely rely on feminist theory developed in the United States, for instance hooks's (1990, 1992) and Wallace's (1990) analyses of cultural politics and race/gender representation, and from Collins's (1990) feminist epistemology, although (some) European women of color may feel uncomfortable with her concept of "Afrocentric feminism." Europe is also quite different from the United States in some crucial aspects.

Europeans have not yet reached the point where they acknowledge and accept that Europe is a continent of natives *and* immigrants. Europeans have not even begun to deal with the problem of racism. Also, different problems emerge with respect to the politics of resistance. Apart from some major European cities, where immigrants from the south represent 20 to 40 percent of the population, the numbers of people of color in Europe are quite small. The fact that we are scattered among different nation-states and deal with different immigration and integration policies hampers cross-national and cross-ethnic organizing. For these and other reasons, European teaching on race, gender, ethnicity, and cultural difference will have to carve out its own space within the European academic world by itself.

I dealt with some of these problems myself in the academic year of 1984–85 when I initiated the first of eight yearly workshops on "Women and Racism" at the then-existing Center for Race and Ethnic Studies at the University of Amsterdam. The course was one of the first, if not the very first, regular course on racism from a woman's point of view. This was one year before my first book on racism in the Netherlands and the United States came out (Essed, 1984, 1990b). The book, based on interviews with black women, challenged the Dutch taboo on questioning Dutch tolerance and on exposing the nature of racism in the Netherlands and, therefore, led to heated debates. In the same period, women of color activists, students, and a few academics, some of whom were affiliated with the white women's movement, started to come out publicly with their anger about racism. Encouraged by the strength emerging from semi-organized resistance, they stood up for themselves, interfered at women's conferences where they felt ignored, and challenged the racism in society at large as well as within the feminist movement (Redmond, 1990).

One does not need too much imagination to visualize the politically and emotionally charged situation of doing a course on "Women and Racism" when this topic is "hot." Yet, rather than adding fuel to the fire, the course was meant to offer a theoretical and explanatory framework for understanding the discourses and lived realities of race, and ethnicity in the Netherlands. Moreover, as the title "Women and Racism" suggests, the course challenged disciplinary boundaries between women's studies and ethnic studies. It was not one of the required courses in the core curriculum, so one could assume that those who chose to participate were motivated to extend their knowledge and understanding in this area.

Since women of color represented not even half of one percent of the student population, it was to be expected that the group would be either completely white or have a majority of white students. Moreover, for many students I was the first woman of color they had ever had as a supervisor. The first meeting of "Women and Racism" was on a Monday afternoon, and of the eight women who joined the session, five were white, two were black. The eighth woman appeared to be white, but many weeks later she started to identify as black. The concept of "black" introduces another essential difference between race and ethnic relations in Europe and the United States.

In Europe, the term "black" is used differently than in the United States, and it has a different meaning. In the United Kingdom, "black" was adopted by emerging coalitions among African-Caribbean and South Asian organizations and activists in the late 1970s and 1980s (Brah, 1992). In the United States, "black" is used only to refer to people of African descent, but the term came to be used in the United Kingdom as a political word to express the common experience of people of color excluded and marginalized on biological/ethnic grounds. In some places and in some cases, the political meaning of the term was stretched even further to include the Irish, because of their experience of colonization, and Turks and Moroccans in the Netherlands because of their discrimination on ethnic grounds. The use of "black" as a political category has always remained, however, controversial. Among other criticisms, the term is said to be construed in essentialist terms and to trivialize the different cultural identities of the various immigrant groups (Gilroy, 1987; Brah, 1992; Anthias & Yuval-Davis, 1992). The problem I have with the notion of identity is its static connotation. In my view one does not *have* identities, let alone just one identity. Neither do "color" and "ethnic" affiliations pertain to mutually exclusive identities. People may relate dynamically to a range of factors. We *identify* with ideas, experiences, purposes, emotions, and so on, on many grounds, including gender, age, region, profession, and ethnicity. In this respect, it is better to speak of *multi-identifications*. Therefore, one can embrace the label of "black" as well as (some aspects of) the ethnic designation of "Surinamese," "East Indian," "Ghanese," "Jamaican," "Dutch," "British," or what have you. Immigrants can feel "black" and identify, on that basis, with a gender and ethnically heterogeneous group because of the shared experience of racial or ethnic exclusion. At the same time, one can also identify with a subgroup on the basis of one or a number of factors including historical specificity, community boundaries, cultural traditions, gender affiliations, and common purposes with respect to the future.

Identifications on one ground can also lead to exclusions on other grounds. During the very first half-hour of that first session on "Women and Racism," one of the black students announced that she was hoping that the group would provide space for her to have separate "all-black" sessions. I knew this woman was involved in the women's movement, and I understood her request as coming from a critique of racism in white women's studies and in the white women's movement (Essed, 1982; Loewenthal, 1984, 1988; Kempadoo & Loewenthal, 1986; Kutluer-Yalim, 1988). Her suggestion to have separate black and white sessions put the issue of race squarely on the table, which caused uneasiness on all sides. The idea of separate groups did not appeal to the other black woman who did not identify at all with feminism. First, some black women disassociate themselves from feminism with the argument that feminists are white and anti-men and that the black women's struggle is in solidarity with black men (see Wallace, 1979; Bulbeck, 1988). Second, she had no desire to discuss "personal" things in seclusion. Because she did not second the proposal, its initiator felt "let down by her own kind." The white women present were looking around a bit scared, guiltily, and somewhat offended, as if they were thinking: We haven't said anything yet and are already rejected for being nonblack. Are we going to be scrutinized and accused of "racism" when we say something "wrong"?

The tension of that situation demonstrates that structural conflict is interwoven in day-to-day interactions and may at any time spark emotions such an angst, anger, and guilt. bell hooks (1984) gives an interesting example of such a situation involving a "young Chicana woman who could pass for White who was a student in class" and who refused to discuss the political implications of the fact that she had the option of switching boundaries between "ethnic" and "white." According to hooks this gave her "a perspective of race totally different from that of someone who is dark-skinned and can never pass." Confronted with this argument, the student "became very angry and finally stormed out of class." hooks recalled that the whole class turned against her for having been too harsh with the young woman but that the student contacted her "weeks later to share her feelings that she had gained new insights and awareness as a result" of that encounter, which had "aided her personal growth."

There may be many ways to deal with conflict. The specific strategy one opts for depends on a number of factors, including the national or regional context (are emotions usually shown or repressed?), the vulnerability of the parties involved (a black female teacher versus a white student represents two different levels of power: functional versus structural [racial] power); the personalities of the parties involved, and so on. Far from avoiding confrontation in order to keep it "safe," I found that with Dutch students, indirect confrontation worked better than a head-on attack.

For instance, students sometimes used the word "Negro" to refer to people of African descent. This, by the way, is still common practice in Holland. It usually happened in the first or second session. Rather than correcting the student on the spot, I would, somewhere in the course of my lecture that same day, discuss the concept of "Negro" and its racist implications (Robinson, 1983). The message would usually come across right then and there.

In conclusion, the racialized dimensions of social relations affect interactions and experiences on a microlevel. The personal, political, or ideological implications of teaching or studying women's/ethnic studies may be different for black women than for white women. These differences are a fact of the societies we live in and must be made explicit before they can be defied. The context within which racial dimensions are made explicit must, however, be one of shared commitment to a common purpose.

Not only inside, but also outside the universities women are making efforts to find common grounds in the struggle against oppression on the basis of race, ethnicity and/or gender.

Access to University, Recognition of Identity, and Participation in Power Structures

The simultaneous operation of race, gender, ethnic, and class factors has kept the numbers of women of color attending university small. Various studies indicate, however, that those who do succeed to get into university often have great ambitions and may become high achievers (Essed, 1991; Giddings, 1988; Perkins, 1983; Smith, 1982; Wilkerson, 1986). Improving access to university for students of color and recognizing their specificities are easy hurdles compared to the next point, which has to do with power sharing. It is relevant to appoint women of color teachers, irrespective of the composition of the student population, because it is also important that white students should be exposed to the expertise of women scholars of non-European background.

Too often, however, explicit visibility (tokenism) veils underlying practices of exclusion. According to the democratic rules, scholars of color may be invited to attend a university meeting or conference. Nobody will forbid them to speak. Quite the contrary, the democratic principle of tolerance is underscored. Women of color get invited to speak at meetings, at conferences, in political parties. But the crucial point is whether what they say is considered to be of consequence. This may seem a rather trivial point, but one must take into consideration that what really counts at the end of the day is that women of color are part of the authority and decision making at all relevant levels of the organization and implementation of the studies programs and that students of color are as welcome as white students to take the courses offered.

Breaking through Boundaries

Pitfalls of Multicultural Women's Studies

For some, multiculturalism only goes "skin-deep." They pay lipservice to the multi-, inter-, or cross-whatever, by taking it to mean simply education about different cultures. Multiculturalism goes back to Furnivall (1948) who introduced it to describe the colonial society in which different peoples seek their own ends without developing feelings of loyalty to the society as a whole. Today, the notion of cultural pluralism is also frequently used to describe European and United States society as consisting of groups that are culturally distinctive and separate.

The model of cultural pluralism operates through the explicit pursuit of cultural diversity, but without questioning the status quo of the dominant culture. When processes of racial and ethnic dominance are not being questioned, a discourse developing around notions of cultural diversity is likely to lead to (a) the objectification of "otherness," (b) the institutionalization of the idea that managing ethnic diversity is the main point of dealing with race and ethnic relations, and (c) the marginalization of elements in society perceived as "ethnic." If multicultural policies are implemented under these conditions, it can only mean that culturally different elements are squeezed into the existing social order. (I discussed this in Chapter 1.)

Taking into account the many criticisms of multiculturalism, various authors argue that multiculturalism must be *transformative*, meaning that multiculturalism cannot be maintained within dominance (Gordon & Lubiano, 1992). Others support the idea of a "hybrid culture." In this respect West (1992, p. 329) argues that we must give up the pursuit of "pure" traditions and "pure" heritages. Moreover, global perspectives on race, culture, gender and ethnicity, mutual respect, and understanding of crusades for justice in other northern and southern locations may enable us to foster *transnational identifications.* Rather than locking ourselves into static identities, many of us identify across national or regional boundaries with a range of purposes, values, and cultural ways.

Toward a Global Framework of Women's Studies/Ethnic Studies

During the eight years I presented the workshops on women and racism, the curriculum changed according to the availability of publications on Dutch race relations and racism and according to my personal academic development in the area of concern. At first United States publications dominated the curriculum, and these were later joined by those from the United Kingdom. Only after a number of years, when there were finally enough relevant publications available on the situation in the Netherlands, did these Dutch works constitute a substantial part of the required reading.

Although the English language is not a major obstacle for Dutch students, the use of foreign-language materials had its problems. Sometimes I wonder whether English-language speakers have any idea of what it means for other language speakers to deal with the fact that international usually means "English language" and that the "international market" in the field of women's studies and ethnic studies is dominated by publications in the English language. Students and scholars from countries such as the Netherlands, Denmark, Sweden, Germany, or Italy have to learn a new language in order to be able to communicate internationally.

Sometimes my students complained that they felt alienated by the language and by the concepts emerging out of the particular national contexts in which certain theories were developed. To give an example, the denial of racism hampered Dutch development of theories in this area for a long time. In classroom discussions, students sometimes had to swallow before they could say "black," "race," or "racism" — terms that were used in the English-language articles but that were taboo in Dutch. Yet the students recognized many of the practices referred to as racism in the English-language articles from their own observations or experiences in the Netherlands.

The initial disadvantage caused by the lack of Dutch publications on intersections of race and gender and on the issue of racism turned out to be an advantage in other ways. Students were challenged to think more internationally and to compare local situations with situations elsewhere. They had the opportunity to develop broader horizons with respect to gender, race, and ethnic relations than students who never learn about these topics through another language and the experiences of marginalized groups elsewhere. A final advantage had to do with the broadening of my own scope over the years; I will conclude this chapter with a note on this advantage.

Initially I only included articles from the south in the curriculum for "Women and Racism" when addressing historical locations of slavery, colonialism, and imperialism. Doing so, however, I also became more sensitive to the international relations of power operating through race and gender today. When millions of people in the south are dislocated due to hunger, wars, or ethnic conflict and when thousands migrate to the north, we must account for these developments theoretically and include critical insights emanating from research in the south into our teaching programs. We can hardly afford to disconnect the issue of race and gender in Europe from the global context when European anti-Islamic sentiments warn — sometimes quite explicitly — white women against the "danger" of Islam from the south "encroaching upon" Europe. Moreover, hostility and aggression against "old" and "new" emigrants from the south place race, racism, and ethnic diversity at the heart of Europe, a declining world power desperately seeking to hold on to the remnants of its previous glory.

11

Cross-Ethnic Coalition Building
A Challenge to Leadership

Recently, I was asked to participate in a workshop organized by Iranian refugee women, most of whom had been in the Netherlands for less than five years. I welcomed the opportunity, because I always learn when I exchange information and experiences with refugee women. My own family had migrated to the Netherlands more than twenty-five years ago under quite different circumstances. And although the experience of each refugee woman is unique in its particular details, many of the stories are also similar to those of first- and second-generation women of the so-called established ethnic minority groups (Essed, 1990a and b, 1991; Lutz, 1991).

There were twenty women and the majority of them had been to college. But only two of them have been able to get jobs in the Netherlands. In everyday life, they are constantly reminded that they are non-European and that they do not belong in the Netherlands. To give a few examples:

One woman, whom I shall call Farah, lives with her ten-year-old daughter in a small Dutch village where they are terrorized by a group of four youngsters who call them in the middle of the night, bang on the front door, harass them in the street, and shout abusive language. The other day, the tires of their bicycles were cut and they found feces in their mail box. Farah knows the reason why. The social worker she has turned to for help knows. The medical doctor she went to see because she developed sleeping problems knows. The local housing agency,

This chapter is a revised version of "Gender, Migration and Cross-Ethnic Coalition Building," published in H. Lutz, A. Phoenix, and N. Yuval-Davis, eds., *Crossfires. Nationalism, Racism, and Gender in Europe* (London: Pluto Press, 1995), pp. 48–64.

which has offered assistance in finding them another place also knows. Even the local policeman knows; one of the youngsters is his nephew. But the taboo against naming the problem is so strong that it does not get called what it is: Racism.

Farah has not yet been in the Netherlands for five years, but she has already learned that the majority resents it if the issue of racism is brought up (Essed, 1991; van Dijk, 1993). She feels repressed when she finds that the consensus shows more understanding of and tolerance for ethnic prejudice and discrimination than for individuals like her. She wants to pinpoint the act, name the problem, and protest against it. Despite being cautioned against pursuing the matter, she refuses to be silenced.

The seven-year-old daughter of another woman, "Soraya," is being harassed by her peer group in school. The daughter is ridiculed for being a "darkie." Pupils spit at her and they pull her hair. At first, Soraya did not know what to do, but then she thought of explaining to her daughter that the white children are jealous of her beautiful dark eyes and her abundant black hair. According to Soraya this has helped. Her daughter has been able to maintain her self-confidence.

It takes courage, will power, and an enormous amount of internal strength to flee, let alone to undertake the journey alone, as Farah and Soraya did. They had hoped to find safety in the Netherlands. Once refugees have obtained a permit to stay, they are expected to adapt to the Dutch way of life, but in return the government provides little protection against racism and xenophobia.

These experiences of Farah and Soraya show that earlier distinctions between newly arriving refugees from the south and ethnic minority groups who settled previously are disappearing and that similarities among people of color in an otherwise white Europe are becoming more important. Indications of this development can also be found in the emergence of cross-ethnic networks on local and inter-European levels. Defying the boundaries determined by nationality, ethnicity, and migration history, women search for a common ground of struggle for human rights and dignity. The background and political implications of cross-ethnic coalition building among women are the subject of this final chapter.

Migration

In the first few decades after the end of the Second World War, two main types of migration led to the formation of new ethnically distinct populations in the countries of Western Europe: migration of workers from the poorer and less industrialized European periphery, often through the "guestworker systems," to the more highly developed parts; and migration of colonized populations to the colonial "mother-lands." The period since the 1980s has seen new patterns of migration, including a growing number of refugees and asylum seekers coming from the south to the north, and, within Europe, from the east to the west (Castles, 1993; Castles & Miller, 1993).

In the 1990s, migration has become a central issue in international relations, and a burning problem in many countries (Wrench & Solomos, 1993). Never before have so many people been on the move: due to the collapse of communism in Eastern Europe; the explosion of violent conflict in many parts of the world; economic deprivation; ecological catastrophe; violence of war; or persecution. An increasing number of people faces semipermanent or permanent displacement. Most of the people who are forced to leave their country in search of safety and a better quality of life remain in the same regional areas. During the past decade, an increasing number of migrants and refugees from the south, however, have sought entry to the rich countries of the north. In the course of this process former distinctions between different types of migrants, such as economic migrants, refugees, and illegal workers are collapsing (Castles, 1993). This merging of reasons has consequences for the way European natives, on the one hand, and the so-called established ethnic minority groups, on the other, perceive themselves in relation to the newly arriving immigrants.

European Identity Crisis

Increasing ethnic diversity in the countries in the north is affecting institutions and cultures. To many in the developed countries, the economic restructuring of the world order, the increasing international cultural exchange, the settlement of populations from the south, and the ongoing global migrations have been experienced as a threat to their social and economic security and their sense of national identity. The contemporary search for a European identity is not a new phenomenon, but the particular constellation of global forces in which this process takes place is specific. Thereby, it seems relevant to make a distinction between feelings of Eurocentrism and Europism, both of which are part of European identity. Eurocentrism was a product of the history of conquest and colonization, and of the Age of Europe (Amin,

1989; West, 1993). Ideologies of European superiority, and in particular the idea that Europe is the cradle and the norm for human civilization, typify an extroverted mode of European assertion. Today, a more introverted process of European assertion is taking place. This I will call *Europism*, a form of introspection. Whereas Eurocentrism emerged from the victory of conquest and the "civilization mission," Europism is based in the defeat of Europe, first by the United States, now gradually by the Far East. Five centuries after Columbus put into effect the idea that country borders should be extended without limit in order to include more and more territories, European countries now close their borders in order to exclude the "Other." The Fortress Europe ideology and the bureaucratic machinery operating to create legal, economic, and political boundaries to protect Europe against the rest of the world, in particular the south, can be considered part of the phenomenon of Europism. Economic decline and internal disintegration are giving way to identity crises and the invention of new enemies. There are enemies within: first-, second- and third-generation racial and ethnic minorities; and enemies on the doorsteps: refugees who are seen as pouring in by the millions in order to take advantage of Western European welfare. On a cultural level Europism is manifest in the nostalgia for the past, which people tend to think of as culturally homogeneous, although in fact that is a myth. It is manifest in the tendency to hold on to an idea of nation-state that is discordant with the reality of migration, local diversification, and cultural globalization.

The trend within Europe for relatively small nations to seek statehood on the basis of shared ethnic identity, whether as a response to colonialism or as a response to a perceived threat of incursion, goes hand in hand with the resurgence of nationalism and neo-Nazi groups within Europe and with an emphasis on "quasi-natural" notions of biological descent. The invention, strategic use, and political manipulation of national-ethnic-racial identities by political leaders has specific gender implications. Nationalism nourishes and is nourished by the subordination of women, whether it concerns racial, religious, ethnic, or political fundamentalism (Cock, 1992; Yuval-Davis & Anthias, 1989; Anthias & Yuval-Davis, 1992; Yuval-Davis, 1994a; Moghadam, 1994). The politics through which national and ethnic identities are created are still largely unexplored so are relevant questions in respect to gender: Is the strategic use of national or ethnic identities characteristic of male leadership or of male styles of leadership? If so, what conclusions can we draw from this and what are the consequences for women? Before focusing on the gender of ethnic leaderships, I first outline some of the general gender implications of migration, immigration policies, and ethnic leadership.

Refugees and Immigration Policies in the Netherlands

The majority of people who are seeking refuge from civil wars or ethnic and other conflicts are women, but the majority of those who propagate and organize ethnic violence are men. Yet, in international politics, few have questioned the gender dimension in the production of wars (Enloe, 1988; Elshtain, 1987; Cooke & Woollacott, 1993). I want to emphasize that I do not mean to suggest that only men are the aggressors and that women are always passive victims. There are conflicting images of women in war situations (Vrouwenberaad Ontwikkelings-samenwerking, 1994). Millions of women — mothers, daughters, sisters, and wives — are innocent victims. But some mothers are proud to send their sons to fight ethnic wars, and some women are active agents of violence, for example in former Yugoslavia and in Rwanda. Women are among the crowds who cheer when men violate, torture, and abuse individual members of the perceived enemy group. Despite these images, it seems relevant to recognize the part gender plays in conflict, migrant, and refugee situations as well as in the integration of refugees in new countries and/or in the rebuilding of societies in postconflict situations.

About 30 percent of the annual requests for asylum in the Netherlands are submitted by women (Desta, 1994). Dutch asylum policy makes a distinction between those who have a chance to obtain refugee status and those who do not comply with the Refugee Convention of Geneva. Decisions used to be made within one year, then the time was reduced to thirty days, and recently cut down even further, to twenty-four hours. The twenty-four-hour rule first only applied to green border asylum seekers (those who reach the Dutch borders over land, through Belgium and Germany), but a policy is in the works to have it applied also to refugees arriving at the Amsterdam Schiphol Airport. This policy anticipates the Schengen Agreement, which states that refugees who have been turned down by one of the member states are not accepted by any of the other ones. Time pressure works particularly to the disadvantage of refugees who suffer from trauma and other serious psychological distress, and a large number of these people are women who have been sexually abused before or during their flight. Furthermore, Dutch law acknowledges the so-called toleration rule. Under this, some of the migrants who will eventually be denied asylum but who, for reasons of safety, cannot return to their countries are allowed to stay in the Netherlands for a maximum of three years. In return they must withdraw their request for asylum. Those who fall under this rule are barely tolerated in the Netherlands. They have few or no rights: no right to be reunited with family members, to travel to any of the other European Union states, to pursue further education, or to engage in any form of employment. As Desta (1994) points out, it is difficult enough for refugee women with an "A-status," that is, with full rights and obligations recognized by the UN convention, to cope in the Netherlands, and much harder for anyone with a less secure status. She explains that refugee policies reinforce traditional gender roles. In the short term, taking care of the usual family and household responsibilities may ease the transition to a new situation, because in these roles there is some continuity. In the long run, however, a lack of connection with the world outside of the home contributes to the further isolation of refugee women.

Restrictive migrant, refugee, and remigration policies have gender specific effects. Women, who enter with their husbands or in order to join them, are seen as dependents, not as migrants or refugees in their own right. Therefore, they are refused an independent residence permit. The consequences of this policy are that they face deportation in case of divorce. This dependent status of women who migrate or flee with their families is particularly unfair. Marriages and family life are severely tested under the hard or life-threatening conditions in the home country, during the actual flight, by the strain of finding work in the new country, and with the on-going tensions and frustration associated with each of these traumatic situations. The almost complete dependence upon their partner impedes women from benefiting from equal opportunity regulations and from participating in women's activities.

Refugee women often find themselves in a vulnerable social situation. In the Netherlands, social networks and structures are unavailable or insufficient; for instance, child care provisions for working women are inadequate. Furthermore, refugee women are frequently isolated from or denied access to resources in the economic, political, and social spheres (Desta, 1994). One way for women to break through the isolation of family life is by organizing women's groups. Organizing women's groups can be empowering because it is a way of breaking the silence of lost hopes and frustrations. Together, women can voice wishes and discuss problems and needs that would otherwise remain unsaid.

Gender, Leadership, and Community Struggle

Within the European Union, ethnic minority groups and refugees are divided by national, cultural, and language borders. These people have to learn the languages of the countries in which they reside, in addition to the languages of the countries from which they originate. The so-called European unification, which is putting into effect the idea of Fortress Europe, reinforces the need among ethnic minority and refugee groups for more effective ways of organizing, in order to bridge the gaps of language and culture. The imperative to organize also at cross-ethnic and cross-European levels forms a new challenge to ethnic leadership.

Leadership of ethnic organizations reflects the level of consciousness of the target group as well as the changing circumstances of migration and settlement. At first, many organizations concentrated on issues related to their countries of origin, with the understanding that migrants would return to their countries. Later, the emphasis shifted to social, economic, and political issues in the country of residence. Initially, leaders were individuals who, by their class background and level of education could mediate between migrants and the receiving society. Their position was strengthened by the authorities in the receiving country and by institutions that, in search of interlocutors, turned to these "leaders" and accorded them prestige, thus enhancing their status (Joly, 1987). Another group of leaders consisted of religious men, predominantly Muslim, Hindi, or Christian. With the shifting of politics from remigration to integration, various new types of leaders, often academics and professionals, gained access to political parties in the receiving countries, during the 1980s. The majority of these "ethnic representatives" were men, but various women have also been elected at local, national, and European levels.

Women on the Move: Toward an Inclusive Politics of Organizing

Women have always been active in the European ethnic minority communities, but few, if any, studies have addressed the gender of ethnic leadership in Europe. Women have worked in organizations alongside men, to further the aims and to defend the rights of their people, to facilitate integration into the receiving society, and/or to contribute to the preservation of their identity as an ethnic group (Mullard, Nimako, & Willemsen, 1990; Rex, Joly, & Wilpert, 1987). Yet the leadership of these organizations is usually male dominated. Excluding women from leadership positions presents problems, because male dominance reinforces the existing patriarchal lines both within ethnic communities and within the society at large.

Given the gender exclusiveness of leadership, women chose to form their own groups, either within the existing ethnic organizations or independently. Thereby, women were among the first to cross ethnic boundaries for the purpose of coalition building: in Britain, the Netherlands, Germany, France, and other European countries (Bryan, Dadzie, & Scafe, 1985; Opitz, Oguntoye, & Schultz, 1986/1991; Dooh-Bunya, 1990). There are various reasons for this. First, ethnic minority and refugee women could identify with each other on the grounds of their struggle as women within their own communities, and as the Other in relation to the women's movement. Second, women, because of their exclusion from power positions in ethnic organizations, are suffering less from the effects of divide and rule government politics. Third, because they were excluded from leadership positions women were liberated to a certain degree from ethnic nationalisms and competitive feelings toward other ethnic organizations.

In all fairness to the male-dominated ethnic organizations, it must be said that in the new situation the commonality of experiences in matters of education, housing, immigration laws, and the labor market stimulated the formation of cross-ethnic and cross-national alliances there as well (Ntoane, 1994). It seems, however, that these alliances are more often than not incidental, or single issue coalitions, rather than lasting associations. Women have been pioneers and leaders in the sense of establishing sustainable cross-ethnic organizations — nationally as well as at a European level. Today, associations where women of African, Asian, Latin American, and other backgrounds work together have emerged all over Western Europe (Kraft & Ashraf-Khan, 1994).

Although the specific histories of these organizations are unique, one can identify a certain progress in the nature of women's organizations, which usually reflects the level of consciousness and the orientation toward the future. When the major emphasis was on the return to the country of origin and the politics there, women often organized on the basis of national background. At a later stage, increasing involvement with the economic and social rights in the receiving country motivated women to join forces with others in similar situations. Thus, associations emerged on the basis of regional or continental affiliation (e.g., Caribbean women, African women, Asian women, Mediterranean women). After that, women continued to expand their networking, now, between African, Caribbean, Asian, and Mediterranean immigrants, to integrate the interests of women who came from the former colonies, as well as women who came in the context of labor migration from southern European and North African countries (e.g., Owaad in Britain; Flamboyant in the Netherlands). A number of these cross-ethnic women's organizations have survived over many years (Salimi, 1994; Weldeghiorgis, 1994).

More recently "established" minority women's groups have reached out to newly arriving people, in particular to refugee women. In the absence of sufficient documentation on this issue, I can only judge from my own observations. It appears that women have been in the forefront when it comes to establishing organizations that bring together ethnic, minority, and refugee interests. These cross-ethnic initiatives are politically important because they form a platform to relate problems experienced within the south, which are causing millions of people to flee (e.g., underdevelopment; ethnic and religious wars; military coups; environmental disasters) more directly to problems people from the south are facing in the north (e.g., racial violence; xenophobia; institutionalized discrimination in the job market, in housing, and in education).

Because I am familiar with Dutch cross-ethnic organizations, I will use this context as an illustration of national initiatives before addressing transnational examples. The late 1980s and 1990s witnessed the emergence of a few all-inclusive women's organizations, which explicitly aim to facilitate local cooperation between ethnic minority and refugee women, such as the organization called Zami. Apart from local initiatives, there is one national organization, an umbrella organization, called "TIYE International." According to TIYE documentation, such as their leaflet and their official response to the European "Green Book on Social Policy" (28 March 1994), TIYE operates from an integrationist perspective. They aim to provide ethnic minority and refugee women in Europe with the same access to employment, appropriate working conditions, and control over economic resources as white women have. At the same time, TIYE points out that the notion of women's emancipation should be defined inclusively, to appeal to all women, taking into account cultural or ethnic background. It is worth mentioning that the politics of TIYE do not only claim to promote equality between women from the south in the north. They also seek to promote interaction between north and south, thus making a connection between the struggle of people from the south who live in the north, and the broader development issues in the south.

The global experience of the women's movements has led to the conclusion that gaining access to decision making is crucial for women if they are to influence issues, and this must include access to public office and the administration of laws. In order to facilitate access to existing (white) women's lobby groups, ethnic minority and refugee women have joined forces on inter-European levels, of which the European Black Women's Network is a good example. Officially launched in 1993, the European Black Women's Network emerged from a conference called by a member of the European Green Party, a black woman, in Brussels, in 1991. Martha Osamor, the current chair, summarized the history and aims (1994). The purpose of the conference was to assess the problems ethnic minority women are confronted with and to create a network. Women who attended this conference agreed that their network should be independent of any particular political party. The idea was to form a network of organizations from which a pressure group at the European level could present claims, exchange and evaluate experiences, and reinforce solidarity among women of color from the colonies and former colonies, Turkish and other noncolonized people who moved to the north of Europe in the context of labor migration during the 1960s and 1970s, and refugees of color.

Depending on their legal status (whether they are a national of a member state, have only a temporary residence permit, are a refugee, or are illegally in the country) some women are allowed to participate in European Union organizations and others are not. Because the European Black Women's Network tends to be inclusive rather than exclusive, relevant information can reach those of us who are excluded from participation in European Union organizations. Furthermore, through communication, sharing of information, and mutual support those who are being excluded can also assert influence on the European decision-making processes.

Through meetings, conferences, and personal contacts, the network facilitates communication and exchange of information within the European Union. The network is the beginning of a platform from which to voice the needs of ethnic minority women; to monitor European politics and participate in decision-making processes at all levels of the European policy-making structure; to develop and propose legislative policies, in particular with respect to racism and sexism; and to produce positive images of women of color and women from the south in economic and social life.

TIYE and the European Black Women's Network cooperate with white women's organizations, but they are primarily geared to facilitate the specific needs of minority women and refugees. This is different for the London-based organization Women Against Fundamentalism (WAF), which was organized in the wake of the Rushdie affair (Yuval-Davis, 1994b). In this widely inclusive organization, women from a variety of religious and ethnic organizations (Christians, Jews, Muslims, Sikhs, Hindus, etc.) have joined to struggle against fundamentalist leaderships of all religions, as well as against expressions of racism in the disguise of antifundamentalism.

These and other initiatives provide experimental places where women can face contributions and complexity, share viewpoints, listen to each other, and try to empathize with women who have partially different positionings, knowledge, and experiences. Although it is too soon to evaluate the long-term viability of cross-ethnic, trans-European networking, there is reason to be confident, given the sustainability of the number of national cross-ethnic initiatives. Adding to this optimistic note, it seems not unlikely that the future will show women to be a rich source from which the diverse leaders will emerge that society needs in order to make the world a place worth living in.

References

The English translations of foreign titles have been provided by Philomena Essed.

AIMD (The American Institute for Managing Diversity). (in press). *The 1995 global conference on managing diversity: At the frontier of integrating research and practice.* Atlanta: The American Institute for Managing Diversity.

Allport, Gordon W. (1958). *The nature of prejudice.* New York: Doubleday, Anchor.

Amersfoort, J.M.M. van. (1974). *Immigratie en minderheidsvorming* [Immigration and minority formation]. Samsom: Alphen a/d Rijn.

Amin, S. (1989). *Eurocentrism.* London: Zed Books.

Amos, V., & Parmar, P. (1981). Resistances and responses: The experiences of black girls in Britain. In A. McRobbie & T. McCabe. (Eds.). *Feminism for girls* (pp. 129–148). London: Routledge & Kegan Paul.

Amos, V., & Parmar, P. (1984). Challenging imperial feminism. *Feminist Review, 17,* 3–19.

Anne Frank Foundation & Dubbelman, J. (1988). *Vooroordelen veroordeeld* [Prejudice denounced]. Kampen: Kok.

Anthias, F., & Yuval-Davis, N. (1992). *Race, nation, colour and class and the anti-racist struggle.* London: Routledge.

Arends, J. (1990). *Jonge Turkse vrouwen in het bedrijfsleven* [Turkish young women in private enterprise]. Leiden: COMT.

Arib, K., & Reijmers, E. (1992). *Marokkaanse vrouwen in Nederland* [Moroccan women in the Netherlands]. Leiden: Stichting Burgerschapskunde.

Babel, M., & Hitipeuw, D. (1992). *Langzaam gaan deuren open* [Slowly but surely, some doors are opening]. Amsterdam: Stichting de Maan.

Bel Ghazi, H. (1982). *Over twee culturen, uitbuiting and opportunisme* [About two cultures, exploitation and opportunism]. Rotterdam: Futile.

Bell, W., & Solomos, J. (1990). (Eds.). *Race and local politics.* London: Macmillan.

Benda-Beckmann, K. von, & Leatemia-Tomatala, F. (1992). *De emancipatie van Molukse vrouwen in Nederland* [The emancipation of Moluccan women in the Netherlands]. Utrecht: Jan van Arkel.

Berg, H. van den, & Reinsch, P. (1983). *Racisme in schoolboeken* [Racism in text books]. Amsterdam: SUA.

Berghe, Pierre L. van den. (1967). *Race and racism.* New York: Wiley & Sons.

Bhavnani, K. (1992). *Towards a multicultural Europe?* Amsterdam: Berdardijn ten Zeldam Stichting.

Bloem, M. (1983). *Geen gewoon Indisch meisje* [Not an ordinary Indonesian girl]. Haarlem: in de knipscheer.

Bousquet, B., & Douglas, C. (1991). *West Indian women at war.* London: Lawrence & Wishart.

Bovenkerk, F. (Ed.). (1979). *Omdat zij anders zijn* [Because they are different]. Meppel: Boom.

Bagley, C. (1973). *The Dutch plural society.* London: Oxford University Press.

Balbo, L., & Manconi, L. (1990). *I razzismi possibli* [The possible racisms]. Milaan: Feltrinelli.

Bablo, L., & Manconi, L. (1992). *I razzismi reali* [The real racisms]. Milaan: Feltrinelli.

Bannerji, H., Carty, L., Dehli, K., Heald, S., & McKenna, K. (1991). *Unsettling relations: The university as a site of feminist struggles.* Toronto: Women's Press.

Barkan, E. (1992). *The retreat of scientific racism.* Cambridge: Cambridge University Press.

Barrett, M. (1980). *Women's oppression today.* London: Verso.

Barrett, M., & McIntosh, M. (1985). Ethnocentrism and socialist-feminist theory. *Feminist Review, 20,* 24–47.

Baruch, E., D'Adamo, A., & Seager, T. (1988). (Eds.). *Embryos, ethics and women's rights.* New York: Harrington Press.

Bovenkerk, F. (1984). Nederland Racistisch? [The Netherlands racist?] *Intermediair, 20* (45), 9.

Bovenkerk, F., Bruin, K., Brunt, L., & Wouters, H. (1985). *Vreemd volk, gemengde gevoelens* [Strange people, ambivalent feelings]. Meppel: Boom.

Brah, A. (1992). Difference, diversity and differentiation. In J. Donald & A. Rattansi (Eds.), *'Race,' culture and difference* (pp. 145–162). London: Sage.

Braham, P., Rattansi, A., & Skellington, R. (1992). (Eds.). *Racism and anti-racism.* London: Sage.

Brandt, G. L. (1986). *The realization of anti-racist teaching.* London: Falmer Press.

Breman, J. (1990a). Primitive racism in a colonial setting. In J. Breman (Ed.), *Imperial Monkey Business* (pp. 89–121). Amsterdam: VU.

Breman, J. (1990b). The civilization of racism: Colonial and post-colonial development policies. In J. Breman (Ed.), *Imperial Monkey Business* (pp. 123–152). Amsterdam: VU.

Brent, L. (1973). *Incidents in the life of a slave girl.* New York: Harvest.

Brink, R. van den, Cuartas, J., & Tanja, J. (1988). *Racisme in Frankrijk* [Racism in France]. Amsterdam: De Balie–S. Franke.

Brittan, A., & Maynard, M. (1984). *Sexism, racism and oppression.* Oxford: Blackwell.

Brouwer, L., Lalmahomed, B., & Josias, H. (1992). *Andere tijden, andere meiden* [Different times, other girls]. Utrecht: van Arkel.

Brown, W. (1983). *Black women and the peace movement.* Bristol: Falling Wall Press.

Brunt, E. (1984, October 13). Raar volk [A weird people]. *De Haagse Post.*

Brunt, E. (1985, January 12). Ik ben racistisch, jij bent racistisch [I am a racist, you are a racist]. *NRC.*

Bruyn-Hundt, M. (1988). *Vrouwen op de arbeidsmarkt* [Women in the job market]. Utrecht: Scala.

Bryan, B., Dadzie, S., & Scafe, S. (1985). *The heart of the race.* London: Virago.

Bulbeck, C. (1988). *One world women's movement.* London: Pluto Press.

Bunyan, T. (1991). Towards an authoritarian European state. [Special issue: Europe: Variations on a theme of racism]. *Race & Class, 32* (3), 19–27.

Caraway, N. (1991). *Segregated sisterhood: Racism and the politics of American feminism.* Knoxville: University of Tennessee Press.

Carby, H. V. (1982). White woman listen! Black feminism and the boundaries of sisterhood. In Centre for Contemporary Cultural Studies, *The empire strikes back: Race and racism in 70s Britain* (pp. 212–235). London: Hutchinson.

Carby, H. V. (1987). *Reconstructing womanhood.* New York: Oxford University Press.

Carroll, C. M. (1982). Three's a crowd: The dilemma of the black woman in higher education. In G. T. Hull, P. B. Scott, & B. Smith (Eds.), *All the women are White, all the Blacks are men, but some of us are brave* (pp. 115–128). Old Westbury: The Feminist Press.

Carty, L. (1991). Black women in academia: A statement from the periphery. In H. Bannerji, L. Carty, K. Dehli, S. Heald, & K. McKenna (Eds.), *Unsettling relations* (pp. 13–44). Toronto: Women's Press.

Castles, S. (1984). *Here for good.* London: Pluto Press.

Castles, S. (1993). Migrations and minorities in Europe, perspectives for the 1990s: Eleven hypotheses. In J. Wrench & J. Solomos (Eds.), *Race and migration in Western Europe* (pp. 17–34). Oxford: Berg.

Castles, S., & Miller, M. (1993). *The age of migration: International population movements in the modern world.* London: Macmillan.

Cense, M. (1991). (Ed.). *Allochtone vrouwen op de arbeidsmarkt* [Nonnative women in the job market]. Rotterdam: WEP.

Chase, A. (1980). *The legacy of Malthus. The social costs of the new scientific racism.* Urbana: University of Illinois Press.

Chaudhuri, N., & Strobel, M. (1992). (Eds.). *Western women and imperialism.* Bloomington: Indiana University Press.

Choenni, G. (1993). (Ed.). *(Meer) vrouwen in de politiek* [More women in politics]. Amsterdam: Emanciptiebureau Amsterdam.

Cock, J. (1992). *Women and war*. London: Open Letters.

Collins, P. H. (1990). *Black feminist thought: Knowledge, consciousness, and the politics of empowerment*. Boston: Unwin Hyman.

Cooke, M., & Woollacott, A. (1993). (Eds.). *Gendering war talk*. Princeton: Princeton University Press.

Corbey, R. (1989). *Wildheid en beschaving* [Wildlife and civilization]. Baarn: Ambo.

Cordus, J. (1991). *'zwarte' en migrantenvrouwen gevraagd* [Request for "black" and migrant women]. Rijnmond: VOR.

Cottaar, A., & Willems, W. (1984). *Indische Nederlanders* [The Indonesian Dutch]. Den Haag: Moesson.

Davis, A. Y. (1981). *Women, race and class*. New York: Random House.

Deslé, E., & Martens, A. (1992). (Eds.). *Gezichten van hedendaags racisme* [Images of racism today]. Brussel: VUB Press.

Desta, A. (1994). Female asylum seekers in the Netherlands. In M. Misckke & A. Roerink. (Eds.), *The future: Women and international cooperation* (pp. 25–27). Oegstgeest: Vrouwenberaad Ontwikkelingssamenwerking.

Deug, F. (1990). *En dan ben je pas echt ver van huis* [And that makes you really feel far from home]. Utrecht: Stichting tegen seksueel geweld.

Dijk, T. A. van. (1987a). *Communicating racism*. Beverly Hills, CA: Sage.

Dijk, T. A. van. (1987b). *Schoolvoorbeelden van Racisme* [Textbook examples of racism]. Amsterdam: SUA.

Dijk, T. A. van. (1991). *Racism and the press*. London: Routledge.

Dijk, T. A. van. (1993). *Elite discourse and racism*. Newbury Park: Sage.

Diop, C. A. (1974). *The African origin of civilization*. Westport: Lawrence Hill.

Donald, J., & Rattansi, A. (1992). (Eds.). *'Race,' culture and difference*. London: Sage.

Dooh-Bunya, L. (1990). Movement for the defence of black women's rights. PCR Information, Special Issue. *Women under racism: A decade of visible action* (pp. 25–28). Geneva: WCC.

Ellemers, J. E., & Vaillant, R.E.F. (1985). *Indische Nederlanders en Gerepatrieerden* [Indonesian Dutch and the repatriates]. Muiderberg: Coutinho.

Ellis, C., & Flaherty, M. (Eds.). (1992). *Investigating subjectivity*. Newbury Park: Sage.

Elshtain, J. (1987). *Women and war*. Brighton: Harvester Press.

Emancipatieraad. (1988). *Zwarte en migrantenvrouwen op de arbeidsmarkt* [Black and migrant women in the job market]. Den Haag: Emancipatieraad.

Enloe, C. (1988). *Does khaki become you? The militarization of women's lives*. London: Pandora.

Entzinger, H. B. (1984). *Het minderhedenbeleid* [Minority policy]. Meppel: Boom.

Essed, Ph. (1982). Racisme en feminisme [Racism and feminism]. *Socialities Feministiese Teksten, 7*, 9–40.

Essed, Ph. (1984). *Alledaags racisme* [Everyday racism]. Amsterdam: Sara.

Essed, Ph. (1988). Understanding verbal accounts of racism. *TEXT, 8* (1/2), 5–40.

Essed, Ph. (1989). Black women in white women's organizations. *RFR/DRF* [Resources for Feminist Research, Toronto, Canada], *18* (4), 10–15.

Essed, Ph. (1990a). Black women's perceptions of contemporary racism in the Netherlands. *International Journal of Group Tensions, 20* (2), 123–143.

Essed, Ph. (1990b). *Everyday racism: Reports from women in two cultures* (Cynthia Jaffé, Trans.). Claremont, CA: Hunter House. (Original work published 1984).

Essed, Ph. (1991). *Understanding everyday racism.* Newbury Park: Sage.

Essed, Ph. (1992). Alternative knowledge sources in explanations of racist situations. In M. McLaughlin, M. Cody, & S. Read (Eds.), *Explaining one's self to others: Reason-giving in social context* (pp. 199–224). Hillsdale, NJ: Erlbaum.

Essed, Ph. (1993). *Things they say straight to your face: Socio-political implications of the usage of racist slurs.* Paper presented at the conference on "Others" in Discourse. Victoria University, Toronto, Canada.

Essed, Ph. (in press). Racism, gender, and interventions in organizational culture: Reflections on diversity management and leadership. In M. Marable (Ed.), *Politics and theory.*

Essed, Ph., & Helwig, L. (1992). *Bij voorbeeld: multicultureel beleid in de praktijk* [For example: multicultural policy in practice]. Amsterdam: FNV.

Essed, Ph., & Reinsch, P. (1991a). *Etnische verhoudingen binnen het gemeentevervoerbedrijf Amsterdam* [Ethnic relations in the municipal transport company]. Part One. Interimrapport. Amsterdam: CRES.

Essed, Ph., & Reinsch, P. (1991b). *Interculturalisering: over oude en nieuwe routes bij het GVB* [Intercultural development: On old and new paths at the GVB]. Amsterdam: CRES.

European Parliament. (1985). *Report of committee of inquiry into the rise of Fascism and racism in Europe.* Belgium, Brussels.

European Parliament. (1986). *Zittingsdocumenten* [Session documents]. Serie A, [Series A], Document A2-160/85/rev. + Bijlagen [Appendix] I–IV. Belgium, Brussels.

European Parliament. (1985). *Report of the committee of inquiry into the rise of Fascism and racism in Europe.* Belgium, Brussels.

Evans, S. (1980). *Personal politics: The roots of women's liberation in the civil rights movement and the new left.* New York: Vintage.

Fanon, F. (1967). *Black skins, white masks.* New York: Grove Press.

Fernandez, J. P. (1981). *Racism and sexism in corporate life.* Lexington, MA: Lexington Books.

Fernandez, J. P. (1991). *Managing a diverse work force.* Lexington, MA: Lexington Books.

Ferrier, J. (1985). *De Surinamers* [The Surinamese]. Muiderberg: Coutinho.

Fox-Genovese, E. (1988). *Within the plantation household.* Chapel Hill: University of North Carolina Press.

Frankenberg, R. (1993). *White women, race matters: The social construction of whiteness.* London: Routledge.

Fullbright, K. (1986). The myth of double-advantage: Black female managers. In M. C. Simms & J. Malveaux (Eds.), *Slipping through the cracks: The status of black women* (pp. 33–45). New Brunswick: Transaction Books. 33–45.

Furnivall, J. S. (1948). *Colonial policy and practice.* London: Cambridge University Press.

Giddings, P. (1985). *When and where I enter: The impact of black women on race and sex in America.* Toronto: Bantam.

Giddings, P. (1988). *In search of sisterhood.* New York: William Morrow.

Gilman, S. L. (1985). *Difference and pathology.* Ithaca: Cornell University Press.

Gilroy, P. (1987). *There ain't no black in the Union Jack: The cultural politics of race and nation.* London: Hutchinson.

Goffman, E. (1959). *The presentation of self in everyday life.* New York: Doubleday.

Goldberg, D. T. (1993). *Racist culture: Philosophy and the politics of meaning.* Oxford: Blackwell.

Gordon, T., & Lubiano, W. (1992). The statement of the black faculty caucus. In P. Berman (Ed.), *Debating P.C.* (pp. 249–257). New York: Laurel.

Goudt, M. (1989). (Ed.). *In de gemeenteraad!* [In the municipal council]. Leiden: Stichting Burgerschapskunde.

Guinier, L. (1994). *The tyranny of the majority: Fundamental fairness in representative democracy.* New York: The Free Press.

Gutman, H. G. (1976). *The black family in slavery and freedom.* New York: Random House.

Hall, S. (1981). Racism and reaction. Commission for Racial Equality, *Five views of multi-racial Britain* (2nd ed.). (pp. 23–35). London: C.R.E.

Hall, S. (1986). Variants of liberalism. In J. Donald & S. Hall (Eds.), *Politics and ideology* (pp. 34–69). Milton Keynes: Open University Press.

Harms, J., & Pollman, T. (1982, May 15). In Nederland door omstandigheden [In the Netherlands due to circumstances]. *Vrij Nederland (kleurenkatern), 19.*

Hermans, P. (1991). De beleving van racisme door Marokkaanse jongeren te Brussel [The experience of racism by Moroccan youngsters in Brussels]. *Cultuur en Migratie, 1991* (1), 63–96.

Hine, D., & Wittenstein, K. (1985). Female slave resistance: The economics of sex. In F. C. Steady (Ed.), *The black woman cross-culturally* (pp. 289–99). Cambridge, MA: Schenkman.

Hoch, P. (1979). *White hero, black beast: Racism, sexism and the mask of masculinity.* London: Pluto Press.

Hodge, J. L., Struckman, D. K., & Trost, L. D. (1975). *The cultural bases of racism and group oppression.* Berkeley, CA: Two Riders Press.

Hooghiemstra, B.T.J., & Niphuis-Nell, M. (1995). *Sociale atlas voor de vrouw.* [The woman's social atlas] Vol. 3: *Allochtone vrouwen* [Allochtonous women]. Rijswijk: Sociaal en Cultureel Planbureau.

hooks, b. (1984). *Feminist theory: From margin to center.* Boston: South End Press.

hooks, b. (1989). *Talking back: Thinking feminist—thinking black.* London: Sheba Feminist Publishers.

hooks, b. (1990). *Yearning: Race, gender and cultural politics.* Boston, MA: South End Press.

hooks, b. (1992). *Black looks: Race and representation.* Boston, MA: South End Press.

Hunter, M., Kaufman, M., & Davis, B. (1995). Diversity: Defining a field that embraces research and practice. *AIMD Research Notes 2* (10), 1–4.

IRR (Institute of Race Relations). (1991). Europe: Variations on a theme of racism [Special issue]. *Race & Class, 32* (3).

IRR (Institute of Race Relations). (1992). The new conquistadors. [Special issue]. *Race & Class, 34* (1).

ISIS (Instituut voor Transcultureel Management). (1992). *Wat is transcultureel management?* [What is transcultural management?] Utrecht: ISIS. (unpublished paper)

Jayawardena, K. (1982). *Feminism and nationalism in the third world.* The Hague: ISS.

Joly, D. (1987). Associations amongst the Pakistani population in Britain. In J. Rex, D. Joly, & C. Wilpert (Eds.), *Immigrant associations in Europe* (pp. 62–85). Aldershot: Gower.

Jones, J. (1985). *Labor of love, labor of sorrow.* New York: Basic Books.

Jong, W. de & Verkuyten, M. (1990). *De smalle marges van Positieve Actie.* [The margins of positive action]. Zeist: Kerckebosch.

Jongh, R. de, Laan, M. van der, Rath, Jan. (1984). *FNV'ers aan het woord over buitenlandse werknemers* [Labor union members speak out on foreign workers]. Leiden: Rijksuniversiteit te Leiden. COMT.

Kalpaka, A., & Räthzel, N. (1991). A note on Ausländerfeindlichkeit. [Special issue: Europe: Variations on a theme of racism]. *Race & Class, 32* (3), 149–152.

Kazim, P. (1991). Racism is no paradise! [Special issue: Europe: Variations on a theme of racism]. *Race & Class, 32* (3), 84–89.

Kempadoo, K. (1988). *In the name of emancipation: Some aspects of the impact of positive action on black and migrant women's work in Amsterdam.* (Working paper no. 7). Amsterdam: CRES publication Series.

Kempadoo, K., & Loewenthal, T. (1986). Verbroken verbindingen [Severed connections]. *Tijdschrift voor Vrouwenstudies, 25,* 76–84.

Kibbelaar, P. (in press). Black women's studies and black feminist studies: Towards a transformative approach. In R. Kilson (Ed.), *Black women in the academy: Defending our name 1984–1994/papers from the conference.* New York: Carlson.

Knowles, C., & Mercer, S. (1992). Feminism and antiracism: An exploration of the political possibilities. In J. Donald & A. Rattansi (Eds.), *'Race,' culture and difference* (pp. 104–125). London: SAGE in association with the Open University.

Kouzes, J. M., & Posner, B. Z. (1993). *Credibility.* San Francisco: Jossey-Bass.

Kraft, M., & Ashraf-Khan, R. (1994). (Eds.). *Schwarze frauen der welt: Europa und migration* [Black women of the world: Europe and migration]. Berlin: Orlanda Frauenverlag.

Kutluer-Yalim, Ö. (1988). Migrantenvrouwen en hun strijd [Migrant women and their struggles]. *Flamboyant Nieuwsbrief* (9), 41–59.

Launer, E. (1991). (Ed.). *Frauenhandel* [Traffic in women]. Göttingen: Lamuv-Verlag.

Lawrence, E. (1982). Just plain common sense: The 'roots' of racism. Centre for Contemporary Cultural Studies, *The empire strikes back: Race and racism in 70s Britain* (pp. 47–94). London: Hutchinson.

Lenders, M., & Rhoer, M. van de. (1983). *Mijn God, hoe ga ik doen?* [Oh my God, how am I going to deal with this?]. Amsterdam: SUA.

Lerner, G. (1973). *Black women in white America: A documentary study.* New York: Vintage Books.

Lima, J. da. (1988). *Als de nood hoog is* [When troubles are deep]. Den Haag: Ministerie van Social Zaken en Werkgelegenheid.

Lindsay, B. (Ed.). (1980). *Comparative perspectives of third world women: The impact of race, sex and class.* New York: Praeger.

Lloyd, C., & Waters, H. (1991). France: One culture, one people? [Special issue: Europe: Variations on a theme of racism]. *Race & Class, 32* (3), 49–65.

Loewenthal, T. (1984). De witte toren van vrouwenstudies [The white tower of women's studies]. *Tijdschrift voor Vrouwenstudies, 17,* 5–17.

Loewenthal, T. (1988). Racisme: het relaas van redicivisme en reclassering [Racism: the story of recidivism and rehabilitation]. *Sophia & Co* (pp. 5–24). Nijmegen: KUN.

Louw-Potgieter, J. (1989). Covert racism: An application of Essed's analysis in a South African context. *Journal of Language and Social Psychology, 8,* 307–319.

Lukes, S. (1974). *Power: A radical view.* London: Macmillan.

Lukes, S. (1986). (Ed.). *Power.* Oxford: Basil Blackwell.

Lutz, H. (1991). *Welten verbinden: Türkische sozialarbeiterinnen in den Niederlanden und der Bundesrepublik Deutschland* [Connecting worlds: Turkish social workers in the Netherlands and in Germany]. Frankfurt am Main: Verlag für Interkulturelle Kommunikation.

MacMaster, N. (1991). The 'seuil de tolérance': the uses of a 'scientific' racist concept. In M. Silverman (Ed.), *Race, discourse and power in France* (pp. 14–28). Aldershot: Avebury.

Makhan, B., Bourret, G., Keiserie, C., & Rambocus, S. (1990). *Armoede? Dat nooit!. Veelbelovende Surinaamse meisjes in Nederland.* [Poverty?: Never! Up-and-coming Surinamese girls in the Netherlands]. Den Haag: Warray.

Mangena, O. (1990). Vernieuwende processen in de sociale wetenschappen: methode, theorie en sociale praktijk; naar een theoretische positie in feministisch denken [Innovating processes in the social sciences: Method, theory and social practice: Toward a theoretical position in feminist thinking]. In B. Fontaine, P. Kloos, & J. Schrijvers (Eds.) *De crisis voorbij: persoonlijke visies op vernieuwing in the antropologie* [Beyond the crisis: Personal perceptions on innovation in anthropology] (pp. 117–140). Leiden: DSWO Press.

Marhé, U. (1993). (Ed.). *Vakvrouwen voor het voetlicht* [Women professionals in front of the footlights]. Den Haag: VeM-bureau Den Haag.

Marshall, J. (1984). *Women managers: Travellers in male world*. Chichester: John Wiley.

McLaughlin, A. N. (1990). Black women, identity, and the quest for human-hood and wholeness: Wild women in the whirlwind. In J. M. Braxton & A. N. McLaughlin (Eds.). *Wild women in the whirlwind* (pp. 147–180). London: Serpents' Tail.

Memmi, A. (1965). *The colonizer and the colonized*. Boston: Beacon Press.

Mercer, K. (1986). Racism and transcultural psychiatry. In P. Miller & N. Rose (Eds.), *The power of psychiatry* (pp. 111–142). Cambridge: Polity Press.

Merckx, F., & Fekete, L. (1991). Belgium: the racist cocktail. [Special issue: Europe: Variations on a theme of racism]. *Race & Class, 32* (3), 67–78.

Meulenbelt, A. (1985). *De ziekte bestrijden, niet de patient* [Combatting the disease rather than the patient]. Amsterdam: van Gennep.

Mies, M., & Reddock, R. (Eds.). (1982). *National liberation and women's liberation*. The Hague: ISS.

Moghadam, V. (Ed.). (1994). *Identity politics and women*. Boulder: West View Press.

Mohanty, C. T. (1991). Cartographries of struggle: Third world women and the politics of feminism. In C. Mohanty, A. Russo, & L. Torres (Eds.), *Third world women and the politics of feminism* (pp. 1–47). Bloomington: Indiana University Press.

Mokhtar, G. (Ed.). (1981). *General history of Africa*. Vol. 2: *Ancient civilizations of Africa*. London: Heinemann.

Morrison, A. M. (1992). *The new leaders*. San Francisco: Jossey-Bass.

Morrison, A. M., Ruderman, M. N., & Hughes-James, M. (1993). *Making diversity happen: Controversies and solutions*. Greensboro, NC: Center for Creative Leadership.

Morrison, A. M., White, R. P., Van Velsor, E., & The Center for Creative Leadership. (1987). *Breaking the glass ceiling: Can women reach the top of America's largest corporations?* Reading, MA: Addison-Wesley.

Moynihan, D. P. (1965). *The Negro family, a case for national action*. Washington, DC: Government Printing Office.

Mullard, C. (1984). *Anti-racist education: The three "O's."* London: National Association for Multi-Racial Education.

Mullard, C. (1986). Pluralism, ethnicism and ideology: implications for a transformative pedagogy. Amsterdam: CRES Publication Series. Working Paper No. 2.

Mullard, C., Nimako, K., & Willemsen, G. (1990). *De plurale kubus: een vertoog over emancipatiemodellen en minderhedenbeleid* [The plural cube: Discourse on emancipation models and minority policy]. Den Haag: Warray.

Nalbantoglu, P. (1981). *Aysel en anderen. Turkse vrouwen in Nederland* [Aysel and the others: Turkish women in the Netherlands]. Amsterdam: Sara.

Nalbantoglu, P. (1990). *Wegens emancipatie gesloten* [Closed during emancipation]. Amsterdam: An Dekker.

Nash, J., & Safa, H. I. (Eds.). (1989). *Sex and class in Latin America*. New York: Bergin Publishers.

Nederveen Pieterse, J. (1990). *Wit over zwart* [White on black]. Amsterdam: KIT.

Ntoane, L. C. (1994, March 4–5). *Black leadership: An absolute necessity.* Paper presented for the Sheeba Refreshers Meeting on the theme of Leadership. Driebergen.

Oakley, A. (1974). *The sociology of housework*. New York: Random House.

Olink, H. (1992, August 22). NRC artikel.

Omi, M., & Winant, H. (1986). *Racial formation in the United States*. New York: Routledge & Kegan Paul.

Oomens, M. (1986). Veelwijverij en andere losbandige praktijken [Polygamy and other licentious practices]. In J. Reijs, E. Kloek, U. Jansz, A. de Wildt, S. van Norden & M. de Baar. (Eds.), *Vrouwen in de Nederlandse koloniën* [Women in the Dutch colonies] (pp. 152–171). Nijmegen: SUN.

Opitz, M., Oguntoye, K., & Schultz, D. (Eds.). (1991). *Showing our colors: Afro-German women speak out* (A. Adams, Trans.). Amherst: University of Massachusetts Press. (Original work published in 1986).

Osamor, M. (1994, March 4–5). *Black leadership in politics.* Paper presented for the Sheeba Refreshers Meeting on the Theme of Leadership. Driebergen.

Overall, C. (1989). (Ed.). *The future of human reproduction*. Toronto: The Women's Press.

Paasman, B. (1987). Mens of dier? De beeldvorming over negers in de tijd voor de rassentheorieën [Human being or animal? Images of Negroes in the period before race theories]. In Anne Frank Foundation, *Vreemd gespuis* [Foreign scum] (pp. 92–107). Amsterdam: Anne Frank Foundation.

Parekh, B. (1988). Introduction. [Special issue: New expressions of racism: Growing areas of conflict in Europe]. *SIM* (7), 9–11.

Parmar, P. (1982). Gender, race and class: Asian women in resistance. Centre for Contemporary Cultural Studies, *The empire strikes back: Race and racism in 70s Britain* (pp. 236–275). London: Hutchinson.

Pattynama, P. (1987). Een tekening in zwart en wit [A picture in black and white]. In M. Brügmann (Ed.), *Vrouwen in Opspraak* [Women get talked about] (pp. 104–119). Nijmegen: Sun.

Penninx, R. (1979). *Naar een algemeen etnisch minderhedenbeleid?* [Toward a general policy for ethnic minorities?] WRR report.

Perkins, L. M. (1983). The impact of the "cult of true womanhood" on the education of black women. *Journal of Social Issues, 39* (3), 17–28.

Pettigrew, T. F. (1981). The ultimate attribution error: Extending Allport's cognitive analysis of prejudice. In Elliot Aronson (Ed.), *Readings about the social animal* (3rd ed.) (pp. 299–318). San Francisco: Freeman.

Pettigrew, T. F. (1985). New black-white patterns: How best to conceptualize them? *Annual Review of Sociology, 11,* 329–346.

Pettigrew, T. F., & Martin, J. (1989). Organizational inclusion of minority groups: A social psychological analysis. In J. P. van Oudenhoven & T. M. Willemsen (Eds.), *Ethnic minorities* (pp. 169–200). Amsterdam: Swets & Zeitlinger.

Pheterson, G. (1986). *The whore stigma.* 's Gravenhage: Ministerie van Sociale Zaken en Werkgelegenheid.

Phizacklea, A. (1990). *Unpacking the fashion industry.* London: Routledge.

Pollmann, T. & Seleky, J. (1979). *Istori-Istori Maluku* [The story of the Moluccans]. Amsterdam: De Arbeiderspers.

Quraishy, B., & O'Connor, T. (1991). Denmark: No racism by definition. [Special issue: Europe: Variations on a theme of racism]. *Race & Class, 32* (3), 114–119.

Ramazanoglu, C. (1989). *Feminism and the contradictions of oppression.* London: Routledge.

Redmond, R. (1980). *Zwarte mensen in kinderboeken* [Black people in children's books]. Den Haag: Nederlands Bibliotheek en Lektuur Centrum.

Redmond, R. (1990). *Daar hoor ik ook bij: De zwarte en migranten vrouwen beweging in Nederland* [I belong there too: The black and migrant women's movement in the Netherlands]. Leiden: Stichting Burgerschapskunde.

Rex, J., Joly, D., & Wilpert, C. (1987). (Eds.). *Immigrant associations in Europe.* Aldershot: Gower.

Robinson, C. (1983). *Black Marxism. The making of the black radical tradition.* London: Zed.

Robinson, J. A. (1987). *The Montgomery bus boycott and the women who started it.* Knoxville: University of Tennessee Press.

Robles, E. (1991). *Doen we't samen of niet: Over de samenwerking tussen zwarten en migrantenvrouwen* [Are we working together or not? On cooperation between black and migrant women]. Amsterdam: SOVA/SS.

Roemer, A. H. (Ed.). (1995). *Het vrolijke meisje* [The merry girl]. Amsterdam: Arena.

Rollins, J. (1985). *Between women: Domestics and their employers.* Philadelphia: Temple University Press.

Saghal, G., & Yuval-Davis, N. (Eds.). (1992). *Refusing holy orders: Women and fundamentalism in Britain.* London: Virago Press.

Salimi, R. (1994). Schwarze menschen im land der mitternachtssonne [Black people in the land of the midnight sun]. In M. Kraft & R. Ashraf-Khan

(Eds.), *Schwarze Frauen der Welt* [Black women of the world] (pp. 62–66). Berlin: Orlanda Frauenverlag.

Sansone, L. (1992). *Schitteren in de schaduw* [Sparkling in the shadow]. Amsterdam: het Spinhuis.

Schein, E. H. (1985). *Organizational culture and leadership*. San Francisco: Jossey-Bass.

Schrijvers, J. (1990). Transformatie in feministisch perspectief: naar nieuwe epistemologische uitgangspunten [Transformation from a feminist perspective: Toward new epistemological points of departure]. In B. Fontaine, P. Kloos & J. Schrijvers (Eds.), *De crisis voorbij: persoonlijke visies op vernieuwing in de antropologie* [Beyond the crisis: Personal perceptions on innovation in anthropology] (pp. 69–90). Leiden: DSWO Press.

Schrijvers, J. (1993). *The violence of development: A choice for intellectuals*. Utrecht: International Books and New Delhi: Kali for Women.

Schuster, J. (1992). The state and post-war immigration into the Netherlands: The racialisation and assimilation of Indonesian Dutch. *European Journal of Intercultural Studies, 3* (1), 47–58.

Seidel, G. (Ed.). (1988). *The nature of the right*. Amsterdam: Benjamins.

Sekaran, U., & Kasner, M. (1992). University systems for the 21st century: Proactive adaption. In U. Sekaran & F. T. Leong (Eds.), *Womanpower: Managing in times of demographic turbulence* (pp. 163–191). Newbury Park: Sage.

Sekaran, U., & Leong, F. L. (Eds.). (1992a). *Womanpower: Managing in times of demographic turbulence*. Newbury Park: Sage.

Sekaran, U., & Leong, F. L. (1992b). Womanpower and changing demographics: Introduction. In U. Sekaran & F. L. Leong (Eds.), *Womanpower: Managing in times of demographic turbulence* (pp. ix–xvii). Newbury Park: Sage.

SIM (Studie- en Informatiecentrum Mensenrechten [Netherlands Institute for Human Rights]. (1988). New expressions of racism: Growing areas of conflict in Europe. *International Alert*, SIM Special (7).

Smith, E. J. (1982). The black female adolescent: A review of the educational, career, and psychological literature. *Psychology of Women Quarterly, 6* (3), 261–288.

Smith, S. J. (1989). *The politics of "race" and residence: Citizenship, segregation, and white supremacy*. Cambridge: Polity Press.

Snowden, F. M. (1969). *Blacks in antiquity*. Cambridge, MA: Harvard University Press.

Sokoloff, N. (1992). *Black and white women in the professions*. New York: Routledge.

Solomos, J. (1989). *Race and racism in contemporary Britain*. London: Macmillan.

Solomos, J., Findlay, B., Jones, S., & Gilroy, P. (1982). The organic crisis of British capitalism and race: The experience of the seventies. In Centre for Contemporary Cultural Studies, *The empire strikes back: Race and racism in 70s Britain* (pp. 9–46). London: Hutchinson.

Stam, D. (1988). Van de West naar het Westen. Surinaamse Studentes in Neder-land, 1918–1940 [From the West Indies to the west: Female Surinamese students in the Netherlands]. In T. Loosbroek, U. Jansz, A. de Wildt, M. de Baar, F. de Haan & F. Dieteren (Eds.), *Geleerde vrouwen: Negende jaarboek voor Vrouwengeschiedenis* [Learned women: Ninth yearbook for women's history] (pp. 213–226). Nijmegen: SUN.

Staples, R. (1976). *The black woman in America.* Chicago: Nelson-Hall.

Stember, C. H. (1976). *Sexual racism.* New York: Harper Colophon.

Terry, R. W. (1975). *For whites only* (Rev. ed.). Grand Rapids, MI: Eerdmans.

Terry, W. (1984). *Zwarte soldaten in Vietnam* [Black soldiers in Vietnam]. Utrecht: Veen Uitgevers.

Theunis, S. (1979). *Ze zien liever mijn handen dan mijn gezicht* [They like my hands better than my face]. Baarn: het wereldvenster.

Thomas, R. (1991). *Beyond race and gender: Unleashing the power of your total work force by managing diversity.* New York: AMACOM.

Tichy, N. M., & Devanna, M. A. (1986). *The transformational leader.* New York: Jonh Wiley & Sons.

Tizard, B., & Phoenix, A. (1993). *Black, white or mixed race?* London: Rout-ledge.

Tompson, K. (1988). *Under siege.* Harmondsworth: Penguin.

Uyl, R. den, Choenni, C., & Bovenkerk, F. (1986). Mag het ook een buiten-lander wezen [Will a foreigner also do?] *LBR-series, 2.* Utrecht: LBR [National Office against Racism].

Veenman, J., & Jansma, L. G. (1981). *Molukkers in Nederland* [Moluccans in the Netherlands]. Deventer: van Loghum Slaterus.

Veldman, A., & Wittink, R. (1990). *De kans van slagen. Invloeden van cul-turen en regels op de loopbaan van vrouwen* [Chance of success. The impact of cultures and rules on the career of women]. Leiden: Stenfert Kroese.

Verhaar, O. (1991). *Prima inter pares: Over de voorkeursbehandeling van vrouwen* [Best among equals: about preferential treatment for women]. den Haag: Vuga.

Voukelatou, A. (Ed.). (1989). *Laten we het netjes houden* [Let's keep it proper]. Utrecht: LSOBA.

Vrouwenberaad Ontwikkelingssamenwerking (1994). *On the move: Conflict situations and migration: Consequences for women.* Working Docu-ment produced for the Conference "The future: Women and interna-tional cooperation." Amsterdam, May 27.

Wallace, M. (1979). *Black macho and the myth of the superwoman* (2nd ed.). London: Calder.

Wallace, M. (1990). *Invisibility blues: From pop to theory.* London: Verso.

Ware, V. (1992). *Beyond the pale.* London: Verso.

Wekker, G. (1994). *Ik ben een Gouden Munt* [I am gold money]. Amsterdam: Vita.

Weldeghiorgis, E. (1994). Afrikanische Migrantinnen in Italien [African migrants in Italy]. In M. Kraft & R. Ashraf-Khan (Eds.), *Schwarze Frauen der Welt* [Black women of the world] (pp. 67–70). Berlin: Orlanda Frauenverlag.

Wenden, C. W. De. (1991). North African immigration and the French political imaginary. In M. Silverman (Ed.), *Race, discourse and power in France* (pp. 98–110). Aldershot: Avebury.

Werf, S. van der. (1992). (Ed.). *Allochtonen aan het werk* [Nonnative people at work]. Muiderberg: Coutinho.

West, C. (1992). Diverse new world. In P. Berman (Ed.), *Debating P.C.* (pp. 326–332). New York: Laurel.

West, C. (1993). The new cultural politics of difference. In B. Thompson & S. Tyagi (Eds.), *Beyond a dream deferred* (pp. 326–332). Minneapolis: University of Minnesota Press.

White, D. G. (1985). *Ar'n't I a woman?* New York: Norton.

Wilkerson, M. B. (1986). A report on the educational status of black women during the un decade of women, 1976–85. In M. Simms & J. Malveaux (Eds.), *Slipping through the cracks* (pp. 83–96). New Brunswick: Transaction Books.

Willemsen, G. (1988). Minderheden op de arbeidsmarkt: de gevolgen van een verkeerd geïnspireerde politiek [Minorities in the job market: The consequences of awry inspired politics]. *Migrantenstudies, 4* (1), 50–66.

Wilson, A. (1987). *Mixed race children.* London: Allen & Unwin.

Wrench, J., & Solomos, J. (Eds.). (1993). *Racism and migration in Western Europe.* Oxford: Berg.

Young, I. M. (1990). *Justice and the politics of difference.* Princeton, NJ: Princeton University Press.

Yuval-Davis, N. (1994a). Identity politics and women's identity. In V. Moghadam (Ed.), *Identity politics and women* (pp. 408–424). Boulder: Westview Press.

Yuval-Davis, N. (1994b). Women, ethnicity and empowerment. *Feminism and Psychology, 4* (1), 179–197.

Yuval-Davis, N., & Anthias, F. (1989). (Eds.). *Woman-nation-state.* London: Macmillan.

Zamikrant [Zami journal]. (1992), *1 and 2.* Issued by the Black and Migrant Women's Center Amsterdam.